MUTUAL FUNDS
FIFTY YEARS OF RESEARCH FINDINGS

Innovations in Financial Markets and Institutions

Editor:
Mark Flannery
University of Florida

MUTUAL FUNDS
FIFTY YEARS OF RESEARCH FINDINGS

Seth C. Anderson, Ph.D., CFA
University of North Florida

and

Parvez Ahmed, Ph.D.
University of North Florida

 Springer

Library of Congress Cataloging-in-Publication Data

Anderson, Seth C.
    Mutual funds: fifty years of research findings / Ahmed, Parvez
        p.cm. (Innovations in financial markets and institutions ; 16)
    Includes bibliographical references, endnotes and index.

ISBN 0-387-25307-6   e-ISBN 0-387- 25308-4   Printed on acid-free paper.
ISBN 978-0387-25307-7

Printed in the United States of America.

9 8 7 6 5 4 3 2 1   SPIN 11340027

springeronline.com

To my family – wife Linda and children Lela, Frank, and Richard,
for their support throughout my academic career

\- Seth

To my family – wife Savana and children Inam and Hisham for
their encouragement to undertake this endeavor.

\- Parvez

Table of Contents

PREFACE

Investment companies are the dominant vehicles for channeling the savings of U.S. investors into financial assets, here and abroad. In recent years, the amount of assets under management by these organizations was estimated to be $7 trillion, or about $50,000 for every man, woman and child in the United States.

This book synthesizes the academic research to date on the mutual fund industry. Our primary intent is to make the material efficiently accessible to researchers, practitioners, and investors who are interested in the findings and implications of this line of research. We draw from the most widely cited academic journals including *The Journal of Finance, Journal of Financial Economics, Journal of Financial Services Research,* and others, as well as from practitioner-oriented outlets such as *Financial Analyst Journal* and *Journal of Portfolio Management.*

We wish to express appreciation to Professor Mark Flannery of the University of Florida, who supported our proposal to undertake this work. We also want to thank Jack Rogers and Judith Pforr at Springer for their patience. The completion of the book was greatly facilitated by the editorial work of Linda Anderson. We are most thankful to our patient families.

1. AN OVERVIEW OF MUTUAL FUNDS

1.1 Introduction

Mutual funds are a primary vehicle for channeling the savings of U.S. investors into financial assets. These funds are open-end investment companies that sell shares to the public and invest the proceeds in a diversified pool of securities, which are jointly owned by the funds' investors. Over the past decades mutual funds have grown intensely in popularity and have experienced an annual growth rate of over 16%. In 1940 only 68 mutual funds existed, with 296,000 shareholder accounts investing $0.45 billion in assets. At the end of 2003 the Investment Company Institute reports 8,126 funds with 260 million shareholder accounts investing $7.4 trillion in assets. (See Figures 1&2.) Mutual fund popularity is largely due to the following factors: (1) the ease of buying or selling fund shares, (2) the small minimum investment required, (3) the provision of professional record-keeping, (4) the provision of professional portfolio management, and (5) the availability of a large choice of investment objectives.

As the mutual fund industry has evolved over the years, there have arisen many questions about the nature, operations, and characteristics of the funds themselves. Researchers in both academics and the industry itself have addressed these issues in a wide variety of studies. For example, in a unique venue, Edwards and Zhang (1998) report that money flows into stock and bond funds have little impact on security returns, a contrary finding to what many others believe. In a different vein Falkenstein (1996) reports that funds have a preference for volatile stocks and an aversion to low-price securities, and thus may ultimately impact these sectors' securities' prices. Other fund issues that have attracted more widely-spread investigations are matters of: portfolio performance, expenses, investment style, and fund flows. These issues are the subjects of the chapters that follow in this monograph.   Chapter 2 summarizes the major works in performance-related issues. This is followed by Chapters 3 and 4, which review articles focusing on the issues of expenses and investment style, respectively.   Chapter 5 addresses the issue of fund flows, and Chapters 6 and 7 include an eclectic collection of articles involving a variety of issues ranging from hedge funds to board composition to management turnover.   However, before proceeding to these chapters, we first present a brief history of mutual funds and a review of the highlights of the Investment Company Act of 1940.

Figure 1

Growth of Mutual Funds in the US

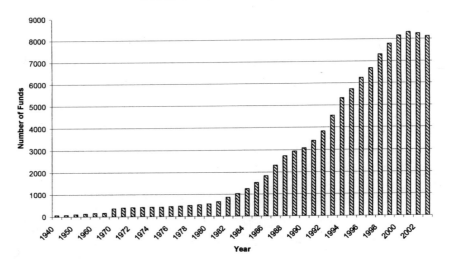

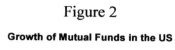

Figure 2

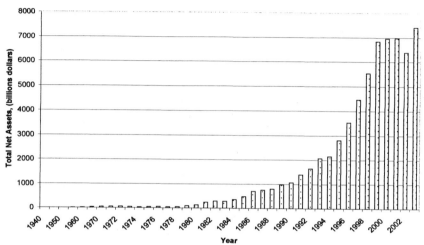

1.2 Historical roots of the mutual fund

European Background

　　In the search for the origins of modern mutual funds some historians look to the closed-end investment trusts developed in Europe in the early 19th century. One of the first investor-owned organizations that pooled and invested primarily in financial assets was *Société Général de Belgique* established by King William I of Belgium. This type of organization gradually took root in Victorian England and Scotland during the mid-1800s. As an example, in 1863 the London Financial Association loaned proceeds from the sale of their shares to domestic railroad companies. The loans were collateralized by securities from railroads, many of which proved to be illiquid, thereby leading to a collapse of the trust. Five years later, the Foreign and Colonial Government Trust sold shares and invested the proceeds in 18 bond issues of foreign countries. Investors in this successful trust received both dividends from their shares and the return of their capital. For the next several years new trusts were formed, usually along similar lines, although such endeavors were infrequent. Dividends were fixed, and the trusts were to liquidate according to their deeds, typically after 20 to 30 years. In 1886 only 12 trusts were listed on the London Stock Exchange. This period of modest growth, however, was followed by an explosion of fund formation and investing.

In the late 1880s the booming economies of the United States, Argentina, and South Africa, presented tempting investment opportunities for the British. Trusts began to invest in mines, plantations, diamond fields, railroads, and real estate. From 1887 to 1890, over 100 trusts were formed. The period was one of high speculation characterized by rising trust share prices, imaginative accounting practices, interlocking directories, exorbitant management fees, and other excesses that forebode a more sober period.

The period 1891-94 was painful for the British investment trust industry. A revolution in Argentina caused a collapse of the South American trust securities. Shortly thereafter, the financial house of Baring failed, creating a panic in every financial center. Security prices went down, and trusts found themselves holding restricted securities bought at high prices as their major assets. Thus began a period of portfolio write-downs, dividend reductions, etc. Although these securities were unpopular with the investing public for many years, the industry later rebounded; today, investment trusts are numerous and extensively traded on the London Stock Exchange.

The American Experience

As to the origins of mutual funds in the United States, some historians look to the Massachusetts Hospital Life Insurance Company, which in 1823 first accepted and pooled funds to invest on behalf of contributors. Yet others refer to the New York Stock Trust (1889) or the Boston Personal Property Trust (1893), which was the first company organized to offer small investors a diversified portfolio as a closed-end investment company. Still other historians hold that the Alexander Fund, established in Philadelphia in 1907, was the forerunner of the modern investment company.

Regardless of the precise origin, the growth of the pure investment company was gradual in the United States. From 1889 to 1924, only 18 investment companies were formed. The trusts had varied purposes, ranging from a near holding company (Railway and Light Securities Company) to an essentially modern closed-end fund (Boston Personal Property Trust). One of these companies, the International Securities Trust of America, became a prototype for later investment trusts in the United States. Organized in 1921, the trust quickly floundered but reorganized in 1923 issuing both bonds and stock. More investment trusts were introduced during the early 1920s, with most of these companies being patterned after British trusts, investing primarily for stable growth, income, and diversification.

However, as shares rose in price and wealth increased, the general public became more enthralled with the stock market. A number of trusts catered to these investors as the 1920s roared on. Eager investors regarded many of the earlier trusts as too conservative, and the popularity of speculative funds exploded. Most of the new funds used substantial leverage in their capital structure. On average, 40% of their capital consisted of bonds and preferred equity. Like most of the investing public, many of these speculative investment companies ignored safety and income considerations, focusing instead on share price appreciation. When the market crashed, many investors lost vast sums of money in these shares. According to a later Securities and Exchange Commission report, by the end of 1937, the average dollar which had been invested in July 1929 in the index of leveraged investment company stock was worth 5 cents while the non-leveraged dollar was worth 48 cents.

Although investments in many investment companies during the 1920s proved to be disastrous, it was in this decade that the first of the modern open-end mutual funds came into existence. Of great importance to the future of the industry was the emergence in 1924 of the first open-end fund, Massachusetts Investors Trust. This fund allowed shareholders to redeem their shares at net asset value, less $2 per share.[1] After the abuses of investment companies during the 1920s, many investors began to seek security in their investments. The redemption policies of open-end investment companies offered a type of security that closed-end investment companies did not have. Also, these companies were unlevered, issuing only stock. From fewer than 20 in number with combined assets of $140 million at the close of the '20s, the new mutual fund-type companies' assets soared to more than $506 million by the end of 1936. During this time the legal and investment environment changed in ways (as seen below) that would foster the growth of the modern mutual fund for decades to come.

Reaction to the Crash

Believing that investment and banking businesses had performed poorly during the Panic, many investors and politicians called for investigations and regulation. The first major piece of legislation, the Securities Act of 1933, set basic requirements for virtually all companies that sell securities. The act requires that publicly traded companies furnish shareholders with full and accurate financial and corporate information. Next, the Securities Exchange Act of 1934 formed the Securities and Exchange Commission (SEC) and gave it broad powers over the investments industry. The act charged the Commission to investigate security trade practices and empowered it to impose accounting and financial standards on interstate broker/dealers and to subject them to periodic inspections.

Soon thereafter, a provision in the 1935 Public Utility Holding Company Act directed the SEC to study investment company practices. Under this provision, investment companies were subject to investigation and regulation. The SEC's investigations ultimately culminated in the Investment Company Act of 1940, which covers the formation, management, and public offerings of investment companies that have more than 50 security holders or that propose to offer securities to the public. The Act of 1940 ended the unrestrained and often unethical practices by which investment companies had been formed, floated, and operated in the United States. Subsequent to the Investment Company Act of 1940, information about the risks, returns, and portfolios held by investment companies has increased and has been standardized. The act is briefly outlined in the following section.

1.3 Investment Company Act of 1940

Management Guidelines

Corporate Entity. The Act of 1940 requires an investment company to be a domestic corporation or a domestic entity taxed as a corporation. This provision rules out personal holding companies attempting to qualify for the "favorable" tax treatment of income under the act. The company must be registered as a management company or a unit investment trust, as defined by the act, at all times during the year when the favorable tax treatment is claimed.

Management Contracts. The investment management franchise cannot be sold to another entity once the company has been chartered. Removal of the investment management contract from the sponsor is possible, provided the motion receives a favorable vote from the shareholders. The investment managers are strictly prohibited from any self-dealing with the firm. In essence, these provisions commit management to a long-term fiduciary obligation to the stockholders, as well as reduce the probability of fraud.

Board of Directors. At least 40% of the Board of Directors must be non-officers or advisors to the fund. Investment brokers or the company's regular brokers may not constitute a majority of the Board. These provisions ensure that a majority of the Board's members are financially independent of the fund.

Investment Policy Guidelines

Income Sources. At least 90% of an investment company's gross income must be passive income (i.e., dividends, interest, and/or gains from the sale of securities). This provision ensures that the non-investment activities of the fund do not contribute to its revenues. For any taxable year, a maximum of 30% of the fund's profits can be derived from the sale of securities held for less than three months (before deducting short-term trading losses, but including all [short- and long-term] gains from the short-sale of securities). This later provision discourages investment companies from speculating on short-term fluctuations in security prices.

Portfolio Composition. The Act of 1940 requires that at the end of each quarter during the taxable year, the fund must: (a) have at least 50% of its assets in cash, cash items (including receivables), government securities, securities of other regulated investment companies, or other financial assets; (b) limit its investment in any single security to 5% or less of its total assets; (c) not have an investment in any single company that represents more than 10% of the outstanding voting securities of the issuer; (d) limit its investment in the securities of any one issuer (except government securities or the securities of other regulated funds) to 25% or less of its total assets; and (e) limit its investment in the securities of two or more controlled (defined as 20% ownership of outstanding voting securities) companies in the same or similar line of business to 25% or less of the total assets of the fund. These restrictions are designed to keep funds from becoming vehicles for controlling other firms or real assets. The Real Estate Investment Trust Act of 1960 provides guidelines for the creation of investment companies that wish to invest in real estate or real estate-based financial assets, paving the way for REITs.

Investment Policy Statement. Upon the initial organization of a fund, or the effective date of the Act of 1940 for funds in existence at that time, a statement of the investment policies and objectives must be provided. This statement addresses in general terms the kinds of financial assets the fund will invest in, the kinds of risks that will be undertaken, the fund's planned use of leverage, etc. Once in place, an investment policy cannot be changed without a majority vote of the shareholders. The purpose of the policy statement is to help potential investors assess the risks they would face as shareholders of the fund, and to ensure that management does not suddenly change these risks.

Capital Structure Guidelines

Minimum Equity Capital. If the firm desires to make a public offering of its common shares, it must have at least $100,000 of equity capital. A prospectus that discloses the information required by the Act of 1940 must accompany any public offering.

Senior Security Limitation. At least three times total assets must cover an investment company's funded debt. At least two times total assets must cover preferred stock issued by the fund. These provisions are designed to create a large margin of safety for the senior security holders of the fund, should it be forced into receivership or bankruptcy.

Tax Policies

If a variety of tests are met, the net profits of investment companies are themselves exempt from federal income taxation. Distribution of income from tax-exempt (taxable) sources is most likely tax-exempt (taxable) for the recipient. The provisions are designed to create an organization that is a "conduit" through which passive income can flow to its shareholders.

Dividend and Interest Income. To retain an investment company's tax-exempt status, a fund must distribute no less than 90% of its net income, exclusive of capital gains. Under the 1950 amendments, dividend and interest income from one fiscal year may be paid in the following fiscal year without jeopardizing the status of the fund. The tax status is maintained as long as the distributions are declared no later than the due date of the fund's tax return and are paid no later than the first regular dividend date following the declaration. Regardless of the source (dividends or interest), distributions are treated as dividend income by the stockholder. These provisions provide funds with an opportunity to delay the declaration and distribution of dividends about one quarter (or a little more if the normal distribution policy of the fund is semi-annual or annual, and the fund follows a calendar fiscal year and files taxes by April 15th).

Capital Gains. To retain an investment company's tax-exempt status, a fund must distribute 100% of net capital gains in a manner and form similar to the one described above. Sub-chapter M of the Act of 1940 permits a fund to retain recognized capital gains without losing its investment company status (and thus, its tax-exempt status on net dividend and interest income). However, electing to retain capital gains leads to a capital gain tax liability that is computed at the maximum possible rate. Although retention is rare, any tax paid by the company would be passed on to stockholders as a tax credit on a pro-rata basis. Clearly this provision is designed to encourage, but not require, funds to be a passive conduit for capital gains.

Types of Investment Companies

Closed-End Funds. Licensed brokers generally offer the shares of a new closed-end fund to the public. Additional offerings of new shares by public closed-end funds are rare. A closed-end fund invests the initial offering's proceeds, less floatation costs, in accordance with the investment policy statement found in the prospectus. Closed-end funds do not continuously engage in a primary offering of common stock. Except for self-liquidating closed-end funds, which are quite rare, the organizations do not have a redemption policy. Changes in ownership of outstanding shares of closed-end funds are undertaken in secondary market transactions, on the exchange (e.g., NYSE) on which the fund's shares are listed.

Open-End Funds. Common shares of an open-end investment company are purchased directly from the fund in a primary market transaction. Purchases may be made through a properly licensed broker, or may be made directly from the fund (e.g., through a dividend re-investment plan). Security regulations require that a prospectus be made available to potential investors prior to the sale. A prospectus is a highly stylized document that contains up-to-date information. The prospectus details the investment philosophy of the fund, assesses the risks of that philosophy, and discloses management fee schedules, dividend re-investment policies, share redemption policies, sales and/or redemption fees, the past performance of the fund, the minimum initial and subsequent investment (dollar) amounts, etc. It is the sale of new shares and redemption policies of open-end funds that distinguish them from closed-end funds.[2]

2. Performance of Mutual Funds

2.1 Introduction

One of the reasons that investors buy mutual funds is the anticipation of investment benefits that portfolio managers may achieve. Ultimately, the performance of the manager must be evaluated in light of the results. However, this seemingly straightforward endeavor is deceptively difficult owing to two principal issues in evaluating fund performance: (1) the choice of benchmark, and (2) the choice of model.

In this chapter we review papers that measure performance and in that process chronicle a four-decades' struggle to reach a consensus on appropriate benchmarks and models for performance evaluation. Thus far, no consensus has been reached. We also review papers that relate to persistence of performance, conditional performance, and market timing. In the following few paragraphs we briefly introduce these related areas of inquiry. The papers summarized in the chapter are listed chronologically at the end of the chapter.

Jensen (1968), Grinblatt and Titman (1989), and Malkiel (1995) are among the principal papers that comprehensively evaluate fund performance. Their results are consistent in showing that actively managed funds do not outperform various broad market benchmarks as evidenced by the negative alphas in Table 2.1.

Although benchmarks are the primary focus of Chapter 4 (Style Analysis), we note here that the work of Lehmann and Modest (1987) is one of the earliest mutual fund papers to stress the critical importance of benchmarking for determining "normal performance." Other earlier related seminal works involving benchmarking include, among others, those of Treynor (1965), Sharpe (1966), and Roll (1978), which are drawn from here.

Table 2.1 – Mutual Fund Performance					
Study	Sample Period	Sample Size	Benchmark	Annualized Alpha	T-Ratio
Jensen (1968)	1945-1964	115	S&P500	-1.10%	-0.69
Grinblatt and Titman (1989)	1974-1984	157	CRSP EW Index	-0.03%	-0.99
Malkiel (1995)	1971-1991	239	Wilshire 500	-0.93%	-1.78

Many studies invoke a Capital Asset Pricing Model (CAPM) framework in performance analysis. Such an approach posits the use of a single portfolio as a benchmark. Treynor, Sharpe, and Jensen each use different proxies for the market portfolio. However, Roll contends that using a single market portfolio as a benchmark is logically inconsistent, as the model assumes that investors have homogeneous expectations. Hence the detection of any abnormal performance can only occur when the market portfolio is inefficient.[3] Thus, given evidence that the usual proxies for the market portfolio are mean-variance inefficient, and that there exist several anomalies such as firm size and P/E ratios, the use of CAPM market proxies as benchmarks is questionable. In a related vein Ross (1976) contends that systematic risk need not be represented by a single factor and instead offers that K factors (where K>1) affect the return of securities. Thus, one of the main contributions of this analysis is the question of whether different constructions of K-factors yield similar or dissimilar measures of performance.

In addition to "pure" performance works, we also review papers addressing persistence of performance. The first major paper to tackle this issue is Hendricks, Patel, and Zeckhauser (1993), who find some evidence of persistence. However, other studies of this phenomenon find that consistency of performance from one period to the next is elusive. For example, in the 1970s the top performing funds were more likely to perform well in the next year than they were likely to do so during the 1980s. Also, some studies conclude that "poor" performers are far more consistent than "good" performers. In summary, some managers can beat the market only some of the time as indicated in Table 2.2.

Table 2.2 – Do Winners Repeat?					
Study	**Sample Period**	**Sample Size**		**Successive Period Performance**	
				Winners	Losers
Goetzmann and Ibbotson (1994)	1976-1988	728	Winners	62%	38%
			Losers	37%	63%
Brown and Goetzmann (1995)	1976-1988	2274	Winners	57%	44%
			Losers	44%	56%
Malkiel (1995)	1971-1991	1047	Winners	65%	35%
			Losers	35%	65%
Kahn and Rudd (1995)	1983-1993	150	Winners	41%	59%
			Losers	59%	41%

The work that best typifies the findings of investigations in this arena is that of Malkiel (1995), who holds that funds have tended to underperform the market both before and after all reported expenses. Other topics addressed in this chapter are those issues of market timing and conditional performance.

Kon (1983) reports that fund managers display some ability to time the market.   However, multivariate tests show that fund managers overall have little or no special information regarding unanticipated market portfolio returns. Jagannathan and Kroajczyk (1986) show theoretically and empirically that portfolios can be constructed to show artificial timing ability when no true ability exists. Thus, the detection of timing is related to the choice of model. As to conditional performance, Ferson and Schadt (1996) advocate a conditional performance model using measures that are consistent with the assumption of a semi-strong form of market efficiency.   Such conditional models allow estimation of time-varying conditional betas, as managers of active portfolios are likely to shift their bets on the market to incorporate information about changing market conditions. We now turn to the papers of interest in chronological order

Close, J., 1952, "Investment Companies: Closed-End versus Open-End," *Harvard Business Review*, 29, 79-88.

Close authored the first academic mutual fund article of which we are aware. In this descriptive work, he discusses the differences between closed-end and open-end funds, and he anticipates many later contributions to the fund literature. Reviewing data on assets under management from 1940 through 1950, the author reports that the open-end portion of the industry passed closed-end funds by the end of 1943. Further, open-end funds (98 of them) had three times the assets of closed-end funds under management by the end of 1950. Close reviews the differences between open- and closed-end funds in an effort to determine if there are any structural reasons for the tremendous growth of open-end funds and the relative stagnancy of closed-end funds.

He argues that the growth in open-end funds is primarily related to the continuous, and well-compensated, sales effort via loads that is undertaken by these funds. In addition, high fixed commission rates on small trades tend to discourage small investments in publicly traded shares, including closed-end funds. Close also contends that the long-standing practice of paying out capital gains by open-end funds could confuse unsophisticated investors.

Close then analyzes the actual investment performance of a sample of open-end funds (37 of the 98 in existence) and the 11 closed-end funds listed on the NYSE. During the period January 1, 1937 to December 31, 1946, and over several sub-periods, the mean NAV returns earned by closed-end fund managers exceeds those earned by the sample of open-end fund managers. Close ends with a caution to potential investors to carefully investigate the expense and management fee arrangements for any fund, open- or closed-end, before committing capital.

Brown, F. and D. Vickers, 1963, "Mutual Fund Portfolio Activity, Performance, and Market Impact," *The Journal of Finance*, 18, 377-391.

Brown and Vickers address the following mutual fund issues: the rates of portfolio turnover, the measurement of performance results, and the impact of trading activity on price formation in the market. The authors reference the findings of their earlier work, "A Study of Mutual Funds" (1962), which investigates the above issues using data from 1953 through 1958. They explain that portfolio performance measures are primarily of interest for shareholders in evaluating a fund's performance relative to its objectives. Market impact has significance insofar as mutual funds can influence conditions in the securities markets. As to portfolio turnover, it is generated by two forces: (1) the investing of new monies received by the fund, and (2) management's decisions to alter the current portfolio.

They report three findings regarding turnover: (1) turnover rates are inversely related to fund size; (2) the distribution of turnover rates is skewed to the right with considerable dispersion; and (3) turnover rates increase in 1954 and 1958, when the market moves upward strongly. As to performance issues, they first explain that the assessment of performance for different types of funds mandates different criteria. However, funds on average perform no better or worse than the composite markets from which they select securities. In addressing market impact, Brown and Vickers attempt to distinguish long-run from short-run effects. At the aggregate security level there is no evidence that funds channel their inflows into common stocks differently in periods of rising markets than in periods of decline. However, there is some evidence of somewhat destabilizing fund activity with respect to individual securities during declining markets. The authors draw two main conclusions: (1) variations in fund portfolio turnover rates are not associated with variations in performance, and (2) fund portfolio activity influences market prices, especially in the short run for individual securities.

Sharpe, W., 1966, "Mutual Fund Performance," *The Journal of Business,* 39, 119-138.

Sharpe's (1966) article is among the earliest research to evaluate the performance of mutual funds using some of the concepts from modern portfolio theory.[4] Sharpe posits that if sound mutual fund management requires the selection of incorrectly priced securities, effective diversification and selection of a portfolio in a given risk class, then there is ample room for major and persistent difference in fund returns.

He explains that the expected return on an efficient portfolio, $E(R_p)$ and its associated risk (σ_p) are linearly related:

$$E(R_p) = R_F + \beta\sigma_p, \tag{1}$$

where R_F is the risk-free rate and β is the premium for risk. If investors can borrow or lend at the risk-free rate R_F and invest in a portfolio with predicted performance of $[E(R_p), \sigma_p]$, then by allocating funds between the risky portfolio and the risk-free asset, an investor can attain any point on the line:

$$E(R) = R_F + \left[\frac{R_p - R_f}{\sigma_p}\right]\sigma. \tag{2}$$

The optimal portfolio will be the one with the greatest reward-to-variability ratio, which is known today as the Sharpe ratio:

$$\left[\frac{R_p - R_F}{\sigma_p}\right]. \tag{3}$$

To test the implication of this formula, Sharpe examines 34 open-end mutual funds spanning a period 1954-1963. There is considerable variability in the Sharpe ratio, with the best and worst performing funds reporting 0.78 and 0.43, respectively.

Sharpe provides two possible explanations for the results: Those who believe in market efficiency may argue that the cross-sectional variation is either transitory or due to excessive expenditure by the funds. Others may attribute the difference to management skills.

The study also examines the persistence of performance. Using measures from the Sharpe ratio and the Treynor index, results indicate that there is some persistence in fund rankings.[5]

Treynor, J. and K. Mazury, 1966, "Can Mutual Funds Outguess the Market?" *Harvard Business Review*, July, 131-136.

Treynor and Mazury discuss the fund manager-investor relationship wherein investors frequently expect managers to be able to anticipate market moves, and the dilemma of whether or not managers should attempt to market time. To address the issue, the authors devise a test of mutual fund historical success in anticipating major moves in the market. They explain that the only way a fund can translate ability to outguess the market into higher returns for shareholders is to vary the fund's volatility systematically in a manner that results in an upwardly concave characteristic line. Rates of return for 57 funds (1953-1962) are employed to investigate whether the volatility of a fund is higher in years when the market does well than in years when the market does poorly. They compute a characteristic line wherein the rate of return for a managed fund is plotted against the rate of return for a suitable market index. There is no evidence of curvature in characteristic lines for any of the funds. From this, they conclude that none of the managers outguess the market and that these managers should not be held responsible for failing to foresee changes in market direction.

Jensen, M., 1968, "The Performance of Mutual Funds in the Period 1945-1964," *The Journal of Finance,* 23, 389-416.

Jensen's is the first work to measure the absolute performance of mutual funds via the introduction of a model that statistically measures a fund's performance relative to a benchmark. His model is a practical adaptation of the Capital Asset Pricing Model (CAPM), which assumes that all investors are risk averse, have homogeneous expectations, and have the ability to choose among portfolios on the basis of their risk and return. The equilibrium model for asset pricing is:

$$E(R_j) = R_F + \beta_j(R_M - R_F),\qquad (1)$$

where R_j = expected return on portfolio j, R_F = risk-free rate of return, β = systematic risk, and R_M = market return. Extending the single period models to allow heterogeneous horizon periods and continuous trading of securities, the model can be generalized to:

$$E(R_{jt}) = R_{Ft} + \beta_j(R_{Mt} - R_{Ft})\ .\qquad (2)$$

The measure of risk β_j is approximately equal to the coefficient b_j in the market model:

$$R_{jt} = E(R_{jt}) + b_j\pi_t + \varepsilon_{jt},\qquad (3)$$

where π_t is the unobservable market factor that affects returns of all securities. It is seen that:

$$R_{jt} - R_{Ft} = \beta_j(R_{Mt} - R_{Ft}) + \varepsilon_{jt}\ .\qquad (4)$$

The risk premium of the jth portfolio is equal to β times the risk premium of the market portfolio plus a random error term. A manager who is a superior forecaster will systematically select securities that have an $\varepsilon_{jt} > 0$. Thus, the portfolio may earn more than its "normal" risk premium for its given level of risk as measured by β. Allowing such forecasting ability implies that a regression must have the possibility of a non-zero intercept. The estimating equation then transforms to:

$$R_{jt} - R_{Ft} = \alpha_j + \beta_j(R_{Mt} - R_{Ft}) + u_{jt},\qquad (5)$$

where the constant "α" is termed Jensen's alpha, while the error term u_{jt} has an expected value of zero and is expected to be serially independent. A positive α is an indicator of an ability to generate superior forecasts of security prices. A negative α is an indication of poor security selection and/or the generation of high expenses as a result of frequent trading or other factors.

Jensen uses data for 115 mutual funds spanning 1945-64 and returns for the S&P 500 index to proxy the market. The funds on average earned 1.1% less that they should have earned given their level of systematic risk. Frequency distributions of the funds show a majority of funds with $\alpha < 0$ and only 39 funds reporting $\alpha > 0$. Thus, on average mutual funds do not produce returns to offset their research expenses and management fees. Jensen also evaluates the statistical significance of α and reports that 14 funds have a t-value less than -2 (negative at the 5% level) while only three funds have performance measures that are significantly positive at the 5% level. Thus, he concludes that there is little evidence that any individual fund does better than mere random chance.

Carlson, R., (1970) "Aggregate Performance of Mutual Funds, 1948-1967," *Journal of Financial and Quantitative Analysis,* 1-32.

The purpose of this paper is to show that the issue of mutual fund performance vis-à-vis the market is influenced by fund type, time period of interest, and market index used. For analysis the author initially employs fund data for the period 1948-1967 to construct indices for three types of mutual funds: diversified stock funds, balanced funds, and income funds. Each index is then compared with three popular market indices. Carlson reports that mutual funds should be grouped by broad investment objectives before asking how they perform relative to the market. In Section II the author shows that regressions of fund returns on Standard &

Poor's composite index returns have a high amount of unexplained variance, which is significantly reduced when a mutual fund index is used as the market proxy. This finding which foreshadows issues of style analysis (see Chapter 4) supports the position that an individual portfolio manager should be compared with an index reflecting actual returns from managed portfolios. Section III investigates several potential determinants of fund performance and finds: (1) past performance is seen to have little predictive value for future performance; (2) net returns during the 1958-1967 decade are not influenced by fund size or expense ratios; and (3) performance is positively related to availability of new cash resources (fund flows) for investment purposes.

McDonald, J., 1974, "Objectives and Performance of Mutual Funds, 1960-1969," *Journal of Financial and Quantitative Analysis,* 311-333.

This work evaluates the objectives and performance of 123 mutual funds using monthly data for the period 1960-1969. The paper considers five questions: (1) Are stated fund objectives related to risk and return? (2) How do funds of differing objectives perform in terms of gross- and risk-adjusted returns? (3) Do average excess returns increase with risk? (4) How does the risk-adjusted performance of the average fund compare to that of the overall market? and (5) Do funds at one end of the risk spectrum outperform those at the other end?

In addressing the above questions, the author initially estimates the systematic risk of each fund by regressing monthly excess returns on market excess returns. Funds are partitioned into six subsets. Initial objectives at the beginning of the decade are found to be positively related both to later measures of beta and total variability. Also, more aggressive portfolios appear to outperform lesser aggressive ones. In analyzing performance characteristics, four measures are examined: (1) Mean monthly excess returns are used as a non-risk-adjusted measure of average return. (2) Mean excess return divided by beta are used as a reward-to-volatility ratio. (3) Jensen's alpha is employed as a measure, and (4) Mean excess return divided by standard deviation is used as a reward-to-variability ratio. The author reports that a majority of the estimated ratios fall below the ratio for the market index. He also reports that the slope of the fund line is not significantly different from that of the market line for the ten-year period. McDonald concludes that, for the mutual fund sample as a whole, the data indicate that funds do not significantly perform differently than the market overall.

Grant, D., 1977, "Portfolio Performance and the 'Cost' of Timing Decisions," *The Journal of Finance*, 32, 837-846.

This work addresses the issue of market timing with regard to: (1) the return attributed to timing, and (2) a previously unspecified "cost" in terms of increased risk. Specifically, the work provides a context for investigating the implications of treating the systematic relative risk of an investment portfolio as a random variable. After a brief review of earlier studies which address mutual fund performance, Grant explains in Section III that the change in risk owing to timing is necessarily unrewarded only if beta and the market return are independent. If they are not independent, the expected return is changed and the portfolio performance may be greater than or less than that of the benchmark. The author compares the performance of a managed portfolio and that of the relative benchmark under the assumption that beta and market return are not independent variables. This section includes a discussion of the potential application of their findings and the role that simulations may play. In Section IV the author contends that neither Jensen's nor Treynor's performance measure is biased because both incorporate the cost of timing decisions. Grant concludes by noting that the relationships investigated are significant both in theory and in application.

Kon, S. and F. Jen, 1979, "The Investment Performance of Mutual Funds: An Empirical Investigation of Timing, Selectivity and Market Efficiency," *The Journal of Business*, 52, 263-289.

In this work the authors employ both the Sharp-Lintner-Mossine (SLM) and Black models of market equilibrium to evaluate mutual fund stock selectivity performance when management is simultaneously engaged in market timing activities. The methodology employed is a switching regression model. Tests of model specification on a sample of 49 mutual funds reflecting different investment objectives find that for many funds a mixture of regressions better fits the data than does a standard linear model. The null hypotheses of risk-level stationarity and of constant selectivity performance are rejected for many individual funds. Many individual funds generate superior selectivity performance for both the SLM and Black models with funds on average selecting superior portfolios. However, both individually and on average, fund managers are unable to select individual securities well enough to recoup research expenses, management fees, and commission costs.

Miller, T. and N. Gressis, 1980, "Nonstationarity and Evaluation of Mutual Fund Performance," *Journal of Financial and Quantitative Analysis*, 15, 639-654.

After a brief review of the revelant mutual fund literature, Miller and Gressis explain that estimates of fund alpha and beta may provide misleading information if nonstationarity is present in the risk-return relationship and is ignored. They present a partition regression and a selection rule to estimate the traditional capital asset pricing model (CAPM) wherein they examine the relationship between the excess rates of return for 28 no-load funds and the excess rate of return for the market. The results suggest only one fund has stationary betas, and the number of betas for any given fund over various periods range upward through ten. They report that their findings indicate some weak, positive relationships and some weak, negative relationships between betas and the market return. They conclude that no significant statistical relationships of either type are found.

Kon, S., 1983, "The Market-Timing Performance of Mutual Fund Managers," *The Journal of Business*, 56, 323-347.

Kon addresses the optimal actions and performance measurement of a portfolio manager who is simultaneously focusing on market-timing and stock selection activity. If a manager believes he can make above average forecasts of portfolio market returns, he will adjust his portfolio risk level ahead of market movements; hence the evidence of systematic risk non-stationarity for a fund is consistent with timing activity. A manager who correctly increases systematic risk above the portfolio target level in anticipation of a bull market will earn an additional return dependent on the risk level shift and the market movement. For empirical purposes Kon employs a sample of 37 mutual funds (Jan. 1960 – June 1976) with objectives of growth, growth and income, balanced, and income. To implement the timing performance estimates for both single period and overall timing, the following are required for each fund: (1) the time series of beta estimates, (2) a proxy for the fund's target beta, and (3) a proxy for the consensus expected return on the market. The results show six funds with positive performance in both timing and selectivity and five funds with positive timing and negative selectivity performance. The sample of funds produces better selectivity than timing performance. Kon concludes that some individual funds display significant timing ability and/or performance. However, multivariate tests show that fund managers overall have little or no special information regarding unanticipated market portfolio returns.

Chang, E. and W. Lewellen, 1984, "Market Timing and Mutual Fund Investment Performance," *The Journal of Business*, 57, 57-72.

In this article the authors employ a parametric statistical procedure that jointly tests for either superior market-timing or security-selection skills to examine the investment performance of a sample of 67 mutual funds during the 1970s. They also briefly discuss several recent studies reporting that mutual funds do not maintain constant risk exposure over time, thus indicating that managers attempt to time the market. These works generally employ a single-factor market model.

Chang and Lewellen employ a market-timing and security-selection test methodology which involves: (1) partitioning the return data into up-market (52 periods) and down-market (56 periods) conditions, (2) estimating the least-squares lines under each condition for every mutual fund, and (3) testing whether the slope-coefficient estimates for the two conditions significantly differ. Using both quarterly and monthly returns series, they find that managers' security selection abilities are significant in magnitude in only five instances out of 67, and three of these five have negative values. Similar statistics are reported for managers' market-timing abilities. None of their results provide evidence of collective portfolio management skill either at the micro- or macro-forecasting level. They conclude that their empirical results are consistent with their model's predictions and that the findings suggest no evidence of skillful market timing or superior security selection abilities.

Jagannathan, R. and R. Korajczyk, 1986, "Assessing the Market Timing Performance of Managed Portfolios," *The Journal of Business*, 59, 217-235.

The authors discuss earlier works which report the puzzling evidence that funds exhibiting significant timing characteristics show negative performance more frequently than positive performance. Jagannathan and Korajczyk demonstrate both theoretically and empirically that portfolios can be constructed to show artificial timing ability when no true ability exists. They propose that certain parametric techniques for determining timing and selectivity performance can yield spurious performance (of the opposite sign) when applied to option-like securities, and offer this as an explanation of funds' tendency to show negative market timing measures. If funds hold assets that are less (more) option-like than the assets in the market proxy, one would expect to see negative (positive) timing measures and opposite signs for measures of security selection.

They propose two methods of testing the specification of market-timing models. The first specification test involves testing linearity by examining the difference between OLS and WLS parameter estimates. The second involves testing restrictions on the coefficients of additional regression independent variables. The tests generally reject linearity when spurious timing is statistically significant. They conclude the work by calling for a useful extension of this analysis involving performance measurements among different mutual fund categories, which may display differences, partially due to artificial timing among groups.

Lehmann, B. and D. Modest, 1987, "Mutual Fund Performance Evaluation: A Comparison of Benchmarks and Benchmark Comparisons," *The Journal of Finance*, 42, 233-265.

In this paper the authors provide empirical evidence on whether the choice of alternative benchmarks has any effect on the measurement of performance. The paper additionally evaluates the efficacy of performance measures that use the standard security market line as a benchmark model.

The model to evaluate fund performance assumes that K-factors affect the returns on individual securities. The return for any mutual fund Rpt can be written as:

$$\widetilde{R}_{pt} = \beta_{pt}\widetilde{R}_{mt} + \varepsilon_{pt} . \qquad (1)$$

The estimate β_{pt} consists of: (1) the average or target sensitivities of the fund to the K common factors, and (2) deviations from the targeted sensitivities by the manager at any given time. The ability to select stocks is reflected in the residual disturbance term, $\varepsilon_{pt.}$ If the manager possesses stock timing ability, then $\varepsilon_{pt} > 0$. In the spirit of Jensen (1968) the regression of R_{pt} on R_{mt} results in:

$$E(R_{pt}) = \widetilde{\alpha}_p + \hat{\beta}_p\widetilde{R}_{mt} . \qquad (2)$$

If a manager does not have superior skills, then the regression equation in (2) will indicate no abnormal performance ($\alpha = 0$). If a fund manager displays superior skills, then $\alpha > 0$. However, a positive alpha may indicate superior stock selection ability but does not provide insight into market timing ability.[6] The authors reformulate Equation (2) to introduce a squared return for the market:

$$E(R_{pt}) = \widetilde{\alpha}_p + \hat{\beta}_{p1}\widetilde{R}_{mt} + \hat{\beta}_{p2}\widetilde{R}_{mt}^2 \,.$$ (3)

In the absence of market timing the coefficient on R_{mt} will be the target beta and the coefficient on R_{mt}^2 will be zero.

The authors construct benchmark portfolios in two ways: (1) for CAPM, CRSP equally-weighted and value-weighted indices of NYSE stocks are used, and (2) for APT benchmarks a two-step process is used. First the sensitivities of the common factors are estimated for a collection of securities, and then in the second step the factor loadings are used to construct the APT portfolios.

Results show that the Jensen measures (α) are sensitive to the choice of APT benchmarks. However, the mean Jensen measures as well as the rankings of funds are insensitive to the choice of the number of common factors (5, 10, or 15). The authors conclude that the choice of a benchmark portfolio may significantly impact performance results and thus is the first crucial step in measuring the performance of a mutual fund.

Grinblatt, M. and S. Titman, 1989, "Mutual Fund Performance: An Analysis of Quarterly Portfolio Holdings," *The Journal of Business,* 62, 393-416.

In contrast to earlier studies which examine the actual returns realized by mutual fund investors, Grinblatt and Titman employ both actual returns and gross portfolio returns of funds in this study. They use this data to estimate survivorship bias and total transactions costs in testing for abnormal returns.

Using quarterly data for the 1975-84 period, the authors calculate Jensen Measures of the funds with four sets of benchmark portfolios: (1) the monthly rebalanced equally-weighted portfolios of all listed CRSP securities, (2) the CRSP value-weighted index, (3) ten-factor portfolios in the spirit of

Lehmann and Modest (1988), and (4) an eight-portfolio benchmark based on firm size, yield, and past returns.

Table 2.3 shows correlations between some variables of interest.

	Expense Ratio [A]	Manage-ment [B]	Turn-over [C]	Hypo-thetical	Actual	Differ-ence [D]
Table 2.3 – Correlation Matrix						
				Jensen Measures		
Net Asset Value	-.35**	-.38**	-.22**	-.18*	-.06	-.16*
Expense Ratio		.17*	.16	.16*	.05	.15
Manage-ment Fee			.34**	.07	-.07	.19*
Log Turnover				.22**	.24**	-.04
Jensen Hypo-thetical					.73**	.32**
Jensen Actual						-.40**

[A] Expenses less management fees as a percentage of net asset value
[B] Stated management fees as a percentage of net asset value
[C] Dollar purchases plus sales as a percentage of net asset value
[D] The difference between the Jensen Measure of the hypothetical return of the fund and its actual return, which is an estimate of transaction costs.
* Significant at .05 level.
** Significant at .01 level.

Important findings include the following: (1) Survivorship bias is on the order of 0.5% annually and is somewhat larger for smaller funds. (2) Transactions costs are on the order of 2.5% annually and are inversely related to the funds' size. (3) Abnormal gross return performance is inversely related to fund size, as are transactions costs, thereby resulting in actual net returns being unrelated to net asset value; and (4) Actual returns do not display positive abnormal returns on average. However, gross returns of both growth and aggressive growth funds are significantly positive on average.

The authors conclude that while superior performance may exist among growth funds, aggressive growth funds, and smaller funds, these funds have the highest expenses, thereby eliminating abnormal investor returns. Thus, investors can not take advantage of the portfolio managers' skills by purchasing shares in these mutual funds.

Grinblatt, M. and S. Titman, 1993, "Performance Measurement without Benchmarks: An Examination of Mutual Fund Returns," *The Journal of Business,* 66, 47-68.

In this article the authors employ the same sample of mutual funds used in their 1989 piece and introduce a new measure of portfolio performance. They note that the Jensen Measure used earlier is subject to criticisms including: (1) sensitivity to the choice of a benchmark portfolio, and (2) introduction of bias in the evaluation of market timers. They explain that the traditional method of portfolio performance evaluation does not employ information that is frequently available about the composition of evaluated portfolios. Here, they employ portfolio holdings with a measure that does not require the use of a standard benchmark portfolio. They proceed from the Event Study Measure that provides an estimate of the time-series co-variances sums between portfolio weights and later returns for each portfolio asset. The Event Study Measure uses future returns as a performance benchmark, which introduce serial correlation in return differences. Grinblatt and Titman's new measure, the "Portfolio Change Measure" requires estimates of the expected weight of portfolio assets, is not subject to survivorship bias, has some statistical computational advantages, and is not subject to the benchmark problems earlier discussed by Roll and others.

When investigating fund holdings for 155 funds (1975-84), they find that performance measures for the groups of funds are similar to the measures found in Grinblatt & Titmann (1989), who use the eight-portfolio benchmark that controls for dividend policy, firm size, and past returns. However, performance measures differ considerably from the other three benchmarks employed earlier.

They conclude that the strongest evidence of abnormal performance is seen in the aggressive growth fund category and that fund performance for both superior and inferior results persists across both halves of the sample. They note that the abnormal portfolio performance documented in their work does not indicate that investors can achieve superior returns by investing in mutual funds because transactions costs and fund expenses essentially dissipate any abnormal investment returns. However, it may be possible for investors to attain abnormal returns by mimicking the portfolios of the superior performing mutual funds.

Hendricks, D., J. Patel, and R. Zeckhauser, 1993, "Hot Hands in Mutual Funds: Short-run Persistence of Relative Performance, 1974-1988," *The Journal of Finance,* 43, 93-130.

The authors employ quarterly returns over 1974-1988 for an initial sample of 165 no-load, growth equity funds, in order to test for short-run persistence. They first establish that excess returns net of management fees exhibit serial correlation. Returns are computed using three benchmarks: (1) single portfolio benchmarks including an equally-weighted index of NYSE equities, (2) an eight-portfolio benchmark similar to that constructed by Grinblatt and Titman (1989), and (3) an equally-weighted index of sample mutual funds.

They find that there is positive performance persistence for four quarters and a reversal thereafter. (Survivorship bias is not considered to be a problem, owing to their sample construction.) They attribute this pattern of returns to possibly an incorrect model specification or to several other likely reasons, including: (1) superior managers get bid away once they build a track record; (2) new funds flow to successful performers leading to a bloated organization and fewer good investment ideas per managed dollar; (3) manager drive is diminished once reputation is established; (4) manager sensitivity is limited to short-term market conditions; and (5) salaries and fees rise in response to recent successes.

The authors rank portfolios into octiles on the basis of the most recent four quarters' returns and find: (1) Mean excess returns increase monotonically with octile rank. A portfolio of better (worse) recent performers does better (worse) in the next quarter. (2) Sharpe's measure, the ratio of mean excess return to standard deviation, also monotonically increases with rank. (3) Jensen's alpha rises monotonically with octile rank, independent of the benchmark used. (4) Estimates of Jensen's alpha are similar across the first set of single portfolio benchmarks, and (5) The evaluation of mutual funds' portfolios is systematically affected by benchmark choice.

The authors confirm their findings of short-term persistence via additional simulations and tests, including another sample of funds for 1989-1990. They also report that "icy hands" occur wherein poor performance persists over time and that this performance is more inferior than "hot hands" performance is superior.

Goetzmann, W. and R. Ibbotson, 1994, "Do Winners Repeat? Patterns in Mutual Fund Return Behavior," *The Journal of Portfolio Management,* Winter, 9-18.

The paper begins with a discussion of the efficient market hypothesis, which implies that excess performance is the result of luck, not skill. The study investigates whether past performance may be used to predict fund relative performance. Three performance issues are addressed: (1) the need for risk adjustment, (2) the issue of survivorship bias, and (3) the dependence of fund returns cross-sectionally.

The authors employ data for 728 mutual funds over the period 1976-1988 and consider two-year, one-year, and monthly gross and Jensen risk-adjusted returns. They find support for the winner-repeat question with both type returns for funds overall, as well as with the relatively homogeneous growth fund subset. Both the top-quartile and lower-quartile performers experience return persistence.

Malkiel, B., 1995, "Returns from Investing in Equity Mutual Funds: 1971 to 1991," *The Journal of Finance,* 50, 549-572.

In a comprehensive study Malkiel employs every diversified equity mutual fund sold to the public for the period 1971-1991 to investigate performance, survivorship bias, expenses, and performance persistence. The author explains that several "cracks" appear in the efficient market edifice during the 1970s and early '80s. Among these for stock returns are: (1) positive and negative correlation among security returns over short and longer time periods, respectively, (2) several seasonal and day-of-the-week patterns, and (3) predictability of stock returns based on variables such as dividend yields, firm size, PE ratios, and price-to-book value ratios. Cracks that appear for mutual funds are: (1) managers' ability to generate returns slightly above the Capital

Asset Pricing Model (CAPM) market line, and (2) past mutual funds returns predict future returns.

Malkiel investigates survivorship bias, performance, performance persistence, and expense ratios, respectively. He reports some impact of survivorship bias as seen in annual returns for all funds of 15.69%, compared to 17.09% and 17.52% for surviving funds and the S&P 500 Index, respectively. These findings contrast with those of Grinblatt and Titman, and Malkiel attributes this to the survivorship bias of those authors' fund sample. To consider performance he calculates the funds' alpha measure of excess performance using the CAPM model.

He finds the average alpha to be - 0.06%, with a T-ratio of only -0.21, thus to be indistinguishable from zero. Using the Wilshire 5,000 Index as a benchmark, he finds the alpha is negative with net returns and positive with gross returns, but neither alpha to be significantly different from zero. He also finds no relationship between betas and total returns. Hence, investors seeking higher returns will generally not obtain them by purchasing high-beta mutual funds.

When investigating the persistence of mutual fund returns, the author analyzes predictability by constructing tables showing successful performance over successive periods. Consistent with earlier studies, he finds that there is some fund return persistence during the earlier decade, but that this persistence does not hold during the second decade. From this he suggests that persistence may have existed earlier, but has since disappeared. However, even when persistence existed during the 1970s, many investors would not have benefited from buying funds with a "hot hand" because of the load charges (up to 8% of asset value) entailed with their purchase.

In his analysis of expense ratios he finds a strong and significant negative relationship between a fund's total expense ratio and its net performance. He does find some evidence that investment advice expenses are associated with positive returns, but attributes this to a few outlying funds, which suggests that investors are not ultimately rewarded for money spent on investment advisory expenses. In the conclusion Malkiel holds that funds have tended to underperform the market both before and after all reported expenses (except loads). Malkiel documents the persistence phenomenon, but notes that it is likely the result of survivorship bias and may not be robust. He concludes that his findings do not provide any reason to abandon the efficient market hypothesis.

Brown, S. and W. Goetzmann, 1995, "Performance Persistence," *The Journal of Finance*, 50, 679-698.

The major contribution of this performance persistence paper is its robust methodology and the use of a data set free of survivorship bias. The authors' analysis of fund data for the period 1976-1988 shows that 1,304 past winners are repeat winners; 1,237 past losers are repeat losers; and 1,936 funds reverse roles. Thus, a majority of funds have persistent performance. However, persistence is not found to be a result of a winning management style each year. Judging performance on an absolute basis in comparison to the S&P 500 Index, the authors report that absolute repeat winners and repeat losers follow approximately the same trend as those of relative repeat winners and losers. It is seen that performance persistence is more likely due to repeat-losers than to repeat-winners, and that poor performance is the strongest predictor of closure.

The table below shows second year returns and alphas for a portfolio strategy where equal amounts are invested in funds ranked by performance in the first year. Top-octile funds do well in the second year; while bottom octile funds do poorly. The results are not sensitive to benchmark choice. Disaggregated results show that previous years' rankings are strong predictors of negative alphas (9 out of 12 years the bottom octile has a negative alpha) but are not necessarily good predictors of positive alphas (7 out of 12 years the top octile has a positive alpha).

Table 2.4 - Summary Statistics for Equally-Weighted Portfolios of Funds in Second Year Ranked by Total Annual Return in the First Year								
	1 Worst	2	3	4	5	6	7	8 Best
Excess Return	1.48	5.23	4.41	5.51	6.48	6.53	7.22	10.17
SD	9.84	12.78	11.21	12.15	13.15	14.88	14.88	17.48
Beta	0.98	1.00	1.01	1.01	1.02	1.02	1.02	1.02
Alpha	-3.98	-0.30	-1.14	-0.01	1.04	0.99	1.65	4.64
	-1.69	-0.17	-0.76	-0.01	0.59	0.51	0.75	1.46

The implication of this paper for investors is that past patterns yield clues about which funds to avoid but do not provide strong indications about which funds will outperform their benchmark in the future. The authors call for future research to address the issues of cross-fund correlations and the persistence of poor performers.

Kahn, R. and A. Rudd, 1995, "Does Historical Performance Predict Future Performance?" *Financial Analysts Journal*, 51, 43-52.

This study uses "style analysis" to stratify funds in order to analyze funds' performance relative to a set of style indices. This contrasts with a single index model, which is used in many earlier works.

The authors employ 300 equity funds and a large sample of taxable bond funds (1983-1993) for analysis. Thirty-six month in-sample data are used to classify the funds' style, and performance is calculated with out-of-sample data. To measure persistence, performance in the out-of-sample period is regressed against the in-sample performance. Persistence would be indicated by positive regression slope coefficients.

Results show no evidence of persistence among equity mutual funds but some evidence of persistence among fixed-income funds. The authors conclude that investors need to include information other than historical performance to select their funds for investments.

Ferson, W. and R. Schadt, 1996, "Measuring Fund Strategy and Performance in Changing Economic Conditions," *The Journal of Finance,* 51, 425-461.

In this paper the authors address the effects of incorporating informational variables in an attempt to more accurately capture the performance of managed portfolios such as mutual funds. Traditional methods of performance evaluation use unconditional expected returns in their models. However, if expected returns and risk vary over time, such an approach is likely to be unreliable.

Ferson and Schadt advocate a conditional performance model using measures that are consistent with the assumption of a semi-strong form of market efficiency. The authors modify the traditional Jensen (1968) model as well as the market timing models of Treynor and Mazuy (1966) and Henricksson and Merton (1981) to incorporate conditioning information. The conditional models allow estimation of time-varying conditional betas, as managers of active portfolios are likely to shift their bets on the market to incorporate information about changing market conditions. During up markets they are likely to increase their exposure to high beta stocks and vice-versa during down markets.

Using 67 mutual funds, over the period 1968-1990, Ferson and Schadt find that risk exposure changes in response to publicly available information about the economy. The use of conditioning information is both statistically and economically significant. Traditional measures of performance produce results with more funds having negative Jensen's alpha than positive. In contrast, Ferson and Schadt's conditional models produce alphas that have a mean value of zero. Also, conditional market timing models remove the evidence of perverse market timing, as suggested by traditional models.

Ferson, W. and V. Warther, 1996, "Evaluating Fund Performance in a Dynamic Market," *Financial Analysts Journal*, 52, 20-28.

The authors explain that common measures of fund performance are unconditional models that use historical average returns to estimate expected performance. Like Ferson and Schadt (1996), this paper also posits that the traditional unconditional models ignore common dependencies between mutual fund betas and expected market returns.

In contrast, the conditional approach includes lagged instrument variables used to represent public information. They present an example that illustrates the efficacy of the conditional model: Assume that the market return in a bull market is 20% and 10% in a bear market. A fund manager holding the market portfolio in the bull market and cash in the bear market, will have its bull market conditional portfolio beta as 1.0, the fund's expected return as 20%, and alpha as zero. Conditional on the bear market, the beta is zero, expected return is equal to the risk-free rate (5%), and alpha is zero. The conditional model correctly evaluates the fund alpha to be zero.

As taken from the paper:

> The unconditional beta of a fund is 0.6. The fund's unconditional expected return is $0.5(0.20) + 0.5(0.05) = 0.125$. The unconditional expected return of the S&P 500 is $0.5(0.20) + 0.5(0.10) = 0.15$, so the fund's unconditional alpha is therefore $(0.125 - 0.05) - 0.6(0.15 - 0.05) = 0.015$. The unconditional approach leads to the mistaken conclusion that the manager has positive abnormal performance.

Ferson and Warther present a conditional or dynamic model which utilizes three factors: the S&P 500 Index, the lagged value of the market dividend yield, and the lagged value of the short-term Treasury yield. These additional factors account for the dynamic strategies followed by many fund managers.

Using monthly returns for 63 funds, the authors' results show that unlike the unconditional models, funds do not routinely underperform the S&P 500 Index on a risk-adjusted basis. The performance is neutral, as would be expected in an efficient market.

Gruber, M., 1996, "Another Puzzle: The Growth in Actively Managed Mutual Funds," *The Journal of Finance*, 51, 783-810.

The growth of mutual funds over the period 1974-1994 has been spectacular with an annual compounded growth rate of 22%. With over $2.1 trillion in investment as of 1994, mutual funds are the second largest financial intermediary in the United States. Equity mutual funds comprise 40% of all mutual funds and own 12.2% of all corporate equity.

Gruber offers four reasons for the popularity of mutual funds: (1) customer service, including record-keeping and the ability to move money into and out of funds easily, (2) low trading costs, (3) diversification benefits, and (4) professional portfolio management.

It is the fourth benefit that distinguishes actively managed funds from passive index funds. Open-end funds sell at net asset value, therefore their pricing does not reflect managerial ability. However, an interesting argument is that management is priced in the long run as superior managers are likely to raise their fees for service.

Gruber uses three measures of abnormal fund performance:

$$R_{it} - R_{mt},\qquad\qquad\qquad\qquad\qquad\qquad\qquad (1)$$

$$R_{it} - R_{ft} = \alpha_i^1 + \beta_{mi}^1(R_{mt} - R_{ft}) + e_i, \text{ and}\qquad\qquad (2)$$

$$R_{it} - R_{ft} = \alpha_i^4 + \beta_{mi}^4(R_{mt} - R_{ft}) + \beta_{si}(R_{st} - R_{lt}) + \beta_{gi}(R_{gt} - R_{vt})$$
$$+ \beta_{di}(R_{dt} - R_{ft}) + e_i\qquad\qquad (3)$$

where equation (1) measures the fund return relative to a market return, equation (2) measures α_i^1 as the excess return from a single index model, and equation (3) measures α_i^4 as the excess return from a four-index model. In these equations R_{it} = return for fund i, R_{mt} = market return, R_{ft} = risk-free return, R_{st} - R_{lt} = difference in return between the small cap and large cap portfolios, R_{gt} - R_{vt} = difference in return between the growth and value portfolios, and R_{dt} - R_{ft} = difference in return between the bond and risk-free portfolios.

Gruber prefers results from equation (3) as the model spans the major types of securities that are usually held by the funds. In addition, to avoid survivorship bias, the paper uses a "follow the money" approach. When a fund changes policy or merges, Gruber assumes that investors place their money in the average surviving funds.

Using a sample of 270 funds for the period 1985-1994, Gruber finds that mutual funds underperform the market by 1.94% per year. With a single index model the underperformance is 1.56%, and with the four-index model the underperformance is 0.65% per year. Nonsurviving funds underperform the market by 2.75% per year, and the average fund's expense is 1.13%. Gruber also tests index funds and finds that they have an average annualized alpha of -20.2 basis points with average expenses of 22 basis points. Finally, the paper also cites some evidence of persistence in performance.

Anderson, S., B. Coleman, D. Gropper, and H. Sunquist, 1996, "A Comparison of the Performance of Open- and Closed-end Investment Companies," *Journal of Economics and Finance,* 20, 3-11.

Reminiscent of Close (1952), Anderson, et al., investigate the impact of fund structure on return performance and related operational characteristics of open-end mutual funds versus closed-end funds. Using a series of regressions and employing a sample of matched open-end and closed-end funds for the period 1984-1993, they test several hypotheses: (1) Mutual fund turnover is greater than closed-end fund turnover; (2) Mutual fund returns are less than closed-end fund returns; and (3) Mutual fund expenses are greater than closed-end fund expenses.

The authors report that both bond and equity open-end funds have higher turnover than do respective closed-end funds. Stock mutual funds tend to outperform stock closed-end funds; whereas bond closed-end funds outperform bond mutual funds. Stock mutual funds have higher expenses than closed-end funds. In contrast, bond mutual funds exhibit lower expenses than bond closed-end funds.

Carhart, M., 1997, "On Persistence in Mutual Fund Performance," *The Journal of Finance,* 52, 57-82.

Following a brief review of earlier works on fund performance persistence, Carhart investigates the persistence issue using a sample of equity funds (free of survivorship bias) from 1962-1993. The sample comprises 1,892 funds divided among aggressive growth, long-term growth, and growth-and-income categories. He employs two models for performance measurement: (1) the Capital Asset Pricing Model, and (2) his four-factor model involving excess returns on a market proxy and returns on factor-mimicking portfolios for size, book-to-market equity, and one-year return momentum.

Initially, portfolios of funds are formed on lagged one-year returns and performance is estimated. With the CAPM model, post-formation excess returns on the decile portfolios decrease monotonically in rank and exhibit an annualized spread of approximately 8%, compared to 24% in the ranking year. In contrast, the four-factor model explains much of the spread among portfolios (the size and momentum factors account for most of the explanation). He reports that expenses and turnover are related to performance with decile ten having higher than average expenses and turnover. It does not appear that fund size, age, or load fees account for the large spread in performance of portfolios. Thus, the strong persistence of short-run mutual fund returns is largely explained by common-factor sensitivities, expenses, and transactions costs.

The author repeats the earlier analyses using two-to-five-year returns in assorted portfolios. Over the longer periods, only top and bottom decile funds maintain their rankings more than would be expected randomly. Decile one funds have a 17% probability of remaining in decile one, and decile ten funds have a 46% probability of remaining in decile ten or disappearing. He concludes that the spread in mean return, unexplained by common factors and fees, is primarily attributable to strong underperformance by funds in decile ten. Expense ratios appear to reduce performance a little more than one-for-one, and turnover reduces performance nearly 1% for every round-trip transaction. The average load fund underperforms no-loads by approximately 80 basis points annually. There is only slight evidence that any mutual fund managers beat the market. Although decile one funds earn back their investment costs, most funds underperform by the amount of their expenses.

Hendricks, D., J. Patel, and R. Zeckhauser, 1997, "The J-shape of Performance Persistence Given Survivorship Bias," *Review of Economics and Statistics*, 79, 161-166.

The authors discuss that social scientists must generally base their inferences on observations of non-experimental information, thereby presenting a challenge to unbiased robust inference from this data. For example, employee competition often eliminates weaker workers, leaving a survivorship bias for those remaining observations. They discuss how Brown et al. (1992) investigate the problems of survivorship bias in assessing the ability of mutual funds (with heterogeneous performance variances) to deliver superior performance. They explain that for groups with performances above the population mean, relative ranks will be positively correlated across sub-periods. Thus, considering all survivorship-biased sample groups, they contend that a spurious j-shaped relation exists between first- and second-period performances.

The authors employ a simple regression-based approach to discriminate between a j-shaped pattern of persistence performance and a monotonic persistence in performance. The method appears to be effective in the simulations conducted. They conclude that mutual funds exhibit a monotonic increasing pattern effected by true performance persistence.

Volkman, D., 1999, "Market Volatility and Perverse Timing Performance of Mutual Fund Managers," *The Journal of Financial Research*, 22, 449-470.

The author investigates fund managers' security-selection and market-timing abilities over the 1980s and performance persistence prior to and after the 1987 crash. To measure managers' selectivity and timing performance, he employs a model incorporating Carhart's (1997) four-factor model and Bhattacharya and Pfleiderer's (1983) quadratic-timing-factor model adjusted for perverse timing performance. Three measures of abnormal fund performance are utilized: Jensen's alpha, Bhattacharya and Pfleiderer's selectivity measure, and an adjusted timing model. He uses monthly net asset values, distributions, fees, loads, and goals for analysis of 332 funds (1980-1990). His findings suggest: (1) the average fund does not exhibit abnormal selectivity performance when assuming either a stationary or a nonstationary risk parameter; and (2) fund managers demonstrate significant perverse timing ability. There is negative correlation between a fund's timing and selectivity performance, which suggests that managers focus on one source of performance to the detriment of the other source. Next, three systematic factors: management compensation, size, and desired risk exposure, are tested for impact on performance. Timing performance is not different between funds with and without incentive fees. Larger funds generate higher returns via security selection, but demonstrate a lack of timing ability. Low-risk funds are more likely to shift from equities to debt in anticipation of declining markets. Lastly, the average fund manager displays no ability to accurately select undervalued investments either before or after the crash of 1987. He concludes that during periods of high volatility few funds correctly anticipate market movements, although many funds outperform the market via security selection.

Becker C., W. Ferson, D. Myers, and M. Schill, 1999, "Conditional Market Timing with Benchmark Investors," *Journal of Financial Economics,* 52, 119-148.

The authors investigate the market-timing ability of mutual funds employing models that: (1) allow the manager's payoff function to depend on excess returns over a benchmark, and (2) distinguish timing based on public information from timing based on superior information. They present a simple model of market timing wherein a manager maximizes single-period utility given a normally distributed private signal about future market returns in excess of a risk-free return. Parameters are estimated that describe the public information environment, the manager's risk aversion, and the accuracy of the fund's market-timing signal.

The authors employ two fund samples (more than 400) from *Morningstar*, which are classified according to objectives: (1) a broad sample of domestic equity funds, and (2) a sample of domestic asset allocation and balanced funds (asset allocators). The initial evidence is reminiscent of prior studies which report "negative" market timing, which makes no economic sense. Hence, they contend that an unconditional model is misspecified, which gives impetus for evaluation of their conditional market-timing model. They follow with several estimates, including an analysis of equity fund groups, asset allocation funds, and portfolio holdings. For all of these, market timing is not a significant factor. In contrast to the unconditional analysis for detecting timing which yields a "wrong" sign, the conditional market timing model removes the negative market timing, but yields no significant evidence of conditional timing. They conclude that their conditional market-timing model yields more reasonable estimates than those reported in the prior literature on market timing.

Lunde, A., A. Timmermann, and D. Blake, 1999, "The Hazards of Mutual Fund Underperformance: A Cox Regression Analysis," *Journal of Empirical Finance,* 6, 121-152.

This paper investigates the relationship between funds' conditional probability of closure and their return performance. The authors explain that the process governing fund attrition rates is important for several reasons: (1) The survivorship bias frequently encountered in the studies of mutual funds is impacted by the average life of funds and their relative performance. (2) The duration profile of funds is important for understanding the incentive environment in which fund managers operate. (3) The termination process might provide information about investor strategies related to poor performance; and (4) Temporal issues of funds closings may provide information on investor assessment of fund performance.

The paper identifies and measures the significance of various factors which influence the process by which, and rate at which, funds are terminated. The authors employ a data set containing monthly returns on a nearly complete sample of U.K. open-ended funds (unit trusts) during the period 1972-1995. The numbers of dead and surviving funds are 973 and 1402, respectively. They initially estimate the hazard and survivor functions nonparametrically. Selected statistics for the rate of fund births and deaths over the period are reported to be approximately 12% and 5%, respectively.

The authors present several reasons why funds are terminated: (1) never reaching critical mass in market capitalization, (2) merging a poorly performing fund with a similar, more successful fund in the same family, (3) merging a poorly performing fund with a similar one after mergers of two fund families, and (4) closing a poorly performing fund to improve family group performance overall. All of these ultimately are related to fund performance, which the authors use to explain fund deaths.

They find that both peer group comparisons and risk-adjusted return comparisons show that negative performance is associated with a higher hazard rate. Since closing funds have higher persistence than funds that survive, excluding them from analysis leads to a decline in persistence estimates. Also, a fund's performance over the past three years is more significant for its closure probability than only its prior year's performance.

Indro, D., C. Jiang, M. Hu, and W. Lee, 1999, "Mutual fund Performance: Does Size Matter?," *Financial Analysts Journal*, 55, 74-87.

In light of Magellan Funds closing its doors to new subscribers in 1997, this paper explores the question: "Does size of fund have any adverse impact on the performance of a fund?"

The authors explain that added economic value can result from having the optimal amount of assets under management. Growth in assets under management can be advantageous because larger transaction volume lowers brokerage commissions. In addition, economies of scale can ultimately impact other costs such as data, research, and administrative expenses.

However, high growth may create some cost disadvantages. Trading large blocks of stocks may result in higher impact costs. Size also draws attention, thus making it difficult for a manager to exploit information asymmetries. Additionally, increased size may result in administrative complexities and may induce the manager to deviate from the fund's stated objectives.

Results from data for 683 funds (1993-1995) show that three-year returns increase as fund size increases. Larger funds have lower expense ratios and lower turnovers. Results from regression analysis yield the following: (1) Funds with higher systematic and unsystematic risk have higher returns; (2) Fund returns are negatively correlated with expense ratios and turnover; and (3) There are diminishing marginal returns from increasing total assets under management. The authors conclude that the optimal fund size for growth, value, and blend funds is approximately $1.4 billion, $0.5 billion, and $1.9 billion, respectively.

Wermers, R., 2000, "Mutual Fund Performance: An Empirical Decomposition into Stock-Picking Talent, Style, Transactions Costs, and Expenses," *Journal of Finance*, 55, 1655-1695.

The majority of past mutual fund performance studies conclude that actively managed funds on average underperform passively managed funds. However, despite such seemingly overwhelming evidence in favor of passive indexing, investors continue to pour large amounts of money into actively managed funds. This paper asks a simple question, "Do mutual fund managers who actively trade stocks add value?"

The author uses a dataset that merges the data from CDA Investment Technologies with the CRSP database. The resulting database provides a complete record of the stock holdings for a given fund, along with turnover ratio, expense ratio, net returns, investment objective, and total net assets under management during each year of a fund's existence. This information allows fund returns to be empirically decomposed into factors attributable to: (1) skills in stock picking, (2) stock holdings, (3) trade-related costs, (4) fund expenses, and (5) differences attributable to other holdings of the fund.

The results of the study indicate that in the past 20 years, growth funds have become the most popular segment of the mutual fund universe and that trading activity in funds doubled from 1975 to 1994. However, the annual trading costs (per dollar invested in mutual funds) in 1994 is one-third their 1975 level. In contrast, the average expense ratio in 1994 is somewhat higher than in 1975.

The author reports that mutual funds on average hold stocks that outperform the market index by 130 basis points per year. This amount roughly equals the expenses and transactions costs combined. On average, funds choose stocks that outperform characteristic benchmarks by 71 basis points per year, but the average net fund return is 100 basis points lower than the CRSP index. Of the 2.3% difference between the return on stock holdings to the net return, about 0.7% is attributable to lower average returns for the non-stock holdings component of the portfolio. The remaining 1.6% is split between expense ratios and transactions costs. High-turnover funds incur significant transactions costs and higher expense ratios, but also hold stocks that have significantly higher average returns than do low-turnover funds. A portion of the higher returns for the high-turnover funds comes from the stock picking skills of the manager. The author concludes that actively managed funds outperform the Vanguard 500 Index on a net return basis.

PAPERS REVIEWED IN CHRONOLOGICAL ORDER

Close, J., 1952, "Investment Companies: Closed-End versus Open-End," *Harvard Business Review*, 29, 79-88.

Brown, F. and D. Vickers, 1963, "Mutual Fund Portfolio Activity, Performance, and Market Impact," *The Journal of Finance*, 18, 377-391.

Sharpe, W., 1966, "Mutual Fund Performance," *The Journal of Business,* 39, 119-138.

Treynor, J. and K. Mazury, 1966, "Can Mutual Funds Outguess the Market?" *Harvard Business Review*, July, 131-136.

Jensen, M., 1968, "The Performance of Mutual Funds in the Period 1945-1964," *The Journal of Finance,* 23, 389-416.

Carlson, R., "Aggregate Performance of Mutual Funds, 1948-1967," *Journal of Financial and Quantitative Analysis,* 1-32.

McDonald, J., 1974, "Objectives and Performance of Mutual Funds, 1960-1969," *Journal of Financial and Quantitative Analysis,* 311-333.

Grant, D., 1977, "Portfolio Performance and the 'Cost' of Timing Decisions," *The Journal of Finance*, 32, 837-846.

Kon, S. and F. Jen, 1979, "The Investment Performance of Mutual Funds: An Empirical Investigation of Timing, Selectivity and Market Efficiency," *The Journal of Business*, 52, 263-289.

Miller, T. and N. Gressis, 1980, "Nonstationarity and Evaluation of Mutual Fund Performance," *Journal of Financial and Quantitative Analysis*, 15, 639-654.

Kon, S., 1983, "The Market-Timing Performance of Mutual Fund Managers," *The Journal of Business*, 56, 323-347.

Chang, E. and W. Lewellen, 1984, "Market Timing and Mutual Fund Investment Performance," *The Journal of Business,* 57, 57-72.

Jagannathan, R. and R. Korajczyk, 1986, "Assessing the Market Timing Performance of Managed Portfolios," *The Journal of Business*, 59, 217-235.

Lehmann, B. and D. Modest, 1987, "Mutual Fund Performance Evaluation: A Comparison of Benchmarks and Benchmark Comparisons," *The Journal of Finance*, 42, 233-265.

Grinblatt, M. and S. Titman, 1989, "Mutual Fund Performance: an Analysis of Quarterly Portfolio Holdings," *The Journal of Business,* 62, 393-416.

Grinblatt, M. and S. Titman, 1993, "Performance Measurement without Benchmarks: An Examination of Mutual Fund Returns," *The Journal of Business,* 66, 47-68.

Hendricks, D., J. Patel, and R. Zeckhauser, 1993, "Hot Hands in Mutual Funds: Short-run Persistence of Relative Performance, 1974-1988," *The Journal of Finance,* 43, 93-130.

Goetzmann, W. and R. Ibbotson, 1994, "Do Winners Repeat? Patterns in Mutual Fund Return Behavior," *The Journal of Portfolio Management,* Winter, 9-18.

Malkiel, B., 1995, "Returns from Investing in Equity Mutual Funds: 1971-1991," *The Journal of Finance,* 50, 549-572.

Brown, S. and W. Goetzmann, 1995, "Performance Persistence," *The Journal of Finance,* 50, 679-698.

Kahn, R. and A. Rudd, 1995, "Does Historical Performance Predict Future Performance?" *Financial Analysts Journal,* 51, 43-52.

Ferson, W. and R. Schadt, 1996, "Measuring Fund Strategy and Performance in Changing Economic Conditions," *The Journal of Finance,* 51, 425-461.

Ferson, W. and V. Warther, 1996, "Evaluating Fund Performance in a Dynamic Market," *Financial Analysts Journal,* 52, 20-28.

Gruber, M., 1996, "Another Puzzle: The Growth in Actively Managed Mutual Funds," *The Journal of Finance,* 51, 783-810.

Anderson, S., B. Coleman, D. Gropper, and H. Sunquist, 1996, "A Comparison of the Performance of Open- and Closed-end Investment Companies." *Journal of Economics and Finance,* 20, 3-11.

Carhart, M., 1997, "On Persistence in Mutual Fund Performance," *The Journal of Finance,* 52, 57-82.

Hendricks, D., J. Patel, and R. Zeckhauser, 1997, "The J-shape of Performance Persistence Given Survivorship Bias," *Review of Economics and Statistics,* 79, 161-166.

Volkman, D., 1999, "Market Volatility and Perverse Timing Performance of Mutual Fund Managers," *The Journal of Financial Research,* 22, 449-470.

Becker C., W. Ferson, D. Myers, and M. Schill, 1999, "Conditional Market Timing with Benchmark Investors," *Journal of Financial Economics,* 52, 119-148.

Lunde, A., A. Timmermann, and D. Blake, 1999, "The Hazards of Mutual Fund Underperformance: A Cox Regression Analysis," *Journal of Empirical Finance,* 6, 121-152.

Indro, D., C. Jiang, M. Hu, and W. Lee, 1999, "Mutual Fund Performance: Does Size Matter?" *Financial Analysts Journal,* 55, 74-87.

Wermers, R., 2000, "Mutual Fund Performance: An Empirical Decomposition into Stock-Picking Talent, Style, Transactions Costs, and Expenses," *Journal of Finance,* 55, 1655-1695.

3. MUTUAL FUND FEES AND EXPENSES

3.1 Introduction

Several empirical studies have explored the link between a fund's risk-adjusted return and expense ratio as well as numerous other related issues. Sharpe (1966) reports that funds with lower expenses have higher reward-to-risk ratios. But Ippolito (1989) finds fund returns to be unrelated to expenses. In addition to these type works, other papers summarized here are those addressing other fund characteristics and performance. Among these are Dellava and Olson (1998) and Dorms and Walker (2001), who examine the relationship of fund performance and fund characteristics such as fees, turnover, and related variables. Their results generally indicate that superior funds have lower costs and that higher turnover activity increases expenses, but not necessarily performance.

Herman, E., 1963, "Mutual Fund Management Fee Rates," *The Journal of Finance*, 18, 360-376.

This work is drawn from the material presented by the author and others in "A Study of Mutual Funds," which was submitted to Congress in 1962.[7] The author initially briefly discusses management fees in regard to fee-related suits of the 1950s – 1960s and then, more in depth, relative to several issues pertaining to management fees paid by the funds, specifically: (1) administrative services provided to the funds, (2) fund performance, and (3) fees and expenses incurred in servicing non-mutual fund clients, among others. The principal findings on fees are as follows: (1) Management fee rates charged to mutual funds by investment advisers approximate one-half of one percent of fund assets. (2) The effective rates charged to non-mutual fund clients are comparably lower than those charged to mutual funds. (3) Management fee rates are less impacted by asset size for mutual funds than for other clients. (4) The variations in fee rates among clients cannot be explained by differences in performance, and (5) Variations in fee rates between mutual funds with advisers and other clients is not explained by differential expenses incurred. The author concludes that where there may be some degree of conflict of interest in areas such as brokerage allocation, turnover policy, and sales effort, the issue of management fee rates raises the question of whether shareholder interests are always best served.

Ferris, S. and D. Chance, 1987, "The Effect of 12b-1 Plans on Mutual Fund Expense Ratios: A Note," *The Journal of Finance,* 42, 1077-1082.

The authors explain that 12b-1 plans are only sales incentives and that they should have no effect on fund management. Their study expands the literature on 12b-1 plans by examining how expense ratios differ in a cross-sectional fund sample. They briefly discuss: (1) loads versus distribution fees, (2) the relative cost of load and no-load funds, and (3) other expense ratio determinants, including fund size, age, objective, and adoption of a 12b-1 plan. To investigate expenses they use a sample of 300 funds for the years 1984-85 and conclude that 12b-1 plans are only a dead-weight cost to investors. They ask why investors are willing to accept this cost and posit this acceptance to: (1) the plan's having been fairly new at the time, and (2) the high likelihood that investors know very little about them.

Starks, L., 1987, "Performance Incentive Fees: An Agency Theoretic Approach," *Journal of Financial and Quantitative Analysis*, 22, 17-32.

In this study the author analyzes and compares two types of incentive contracts for mutual fund managers: "symmetric" contracts vs. "bonus" contracts. Starks' intent is not to explain the *raison d' être* for the contracts, but rather to study their incentive effects. She notes that in 1971 the SEC ruled that contracts have to be symmetric if investment companies use performance-based compensation. However, an earlier study argues that symmetry performance fees do not best serve owner and management interests. Starks' objective is to resolve the issue of incentive compatibility of the two fee schedules. She employs a model wherein a representative portfolio manager invests a sum of money over a single time period for a representative investor and discusses in depth the incentive effects of both type schedules. The potential for fee schedule dependent management-divergent behavior is examined relative to potential agency problems involving: (1) portfolio risk level, and (2) the amount of resources expended on portfolio management. She concludes that the symmetric fee schedule provides appropriate incentives when the managers' decision is to select the portfolio's risk level. However, when considering the managers' decision related to resources spent on portfolio management, the symmetric schedule does not eliminate the agency issue. Although the symmetric fee schedule does not eliminate both potential agency problems, it does dominate the bonus performance fee schedule in regard to agency.

Chance, D. and S. Ferris, 1991, "Mutual Fund Distribution Fees: An Empirical Analysis of the Impact of Deregulation," *Journal of Financial Services Research*, 5, 25-42.

The authors examine the characteristics of funds that implement 12b-1 plans and assess the costs and benefits of such plans. Chance and Ferris discuss the debate within mutual fund and professional circles wherein proponents of 12b-1 plans argue that such plans facilitate payment for services, while opponents contend that the plans represent a deadweight cost.

In this study the authors go beyond the impact of 12b-1 plans on expenses by investigating the differences in age, size, investment policy, objective, and load characteristics of funds with plans, as opposed to those without them. The investigators also consider the impact of plans on management contracts, portfolio liquidity, and turnover, as well as on expenses and investment performance. For analysis they employ data on 306 mutual funds for the years 1984-1988.

Results show that funds adopting 12b-1 plans do not alter their advisory contracts, portfolio turnover, or liquidity, and that in recent years, expense ratios have jumped over 30 basis points because of plans. However, risk-adjusted returns do not appear to be impacted by plan adoption. They conclude that 12b-1 plans should be retained, but that the traditional distinction between load- and no-load funds should be abandoned. Also, they advise that compensation plans should be linked to annual sales rather than to average net assets.

McLeod, R. and D. Malhotra, 1994, "A Re-examination of the Effect of 12b-1 Plans on Mutual Fund Expense Ratios," *The Journal of Financial Research*, 17, 231-240.

The authors explain that proponents of 12b-1 plans often argue that increasing broker selling incentives results in: (1) additional growth which provides economies of scale, (2) continuous inflows for meeting fund redemptions, and (3) an alternative method for investors to pay for services. In contrast, opponents argue that these payments are only concealed sales charges. To resolve the controversy over whether 12b-1 plans are beneficial or harmful, the authors investigate the association between a fund's having a plan and its expense ratio. They employ data from 1988-1999 for a sample of 929 funds and regress the expense ratio on size, growth, income, age, load, and 12b-a plan. They find that larger funds have lower expense ratios due to economies of scale and that the expense ratio is also negatively related to age. Growth and income are not found to be significant variables, and neither is load. However, funds that have a 12b-1 plan have higher expense ratios than funds that do not have a plan. This contributes to the evidence that 12b-1 plans are a deadweight cost to investors over the period of interest. From this, the authors question whether disinterested directors who support 12b-1 plans have acted in the best interest of shareholders, as is their charge.

Kihn, J., 1996, "To Load or Not to Load? A Study of Marketing and Distribution Charges of Mutual Funds," *Financial Analysts Journal*, (May/June), 28-36.

The author briefly discusses the recent acceleration of mutual fund company marketing efforts and then covers the following issues: (1) the variables determining the charging of marketing costs, (2) performance and marketing costs, and (3) the justification of marketing costs. He uses a sample of 2,496 funds over the period 1992-1993 and proposes a model involving the following variables: current marketing charges (up-front load or 12b-1 charges), performance characteristics (return, risk, and asset class), customer services (telephone switching, minimum purchase, etc.), and deferred charges (charges or penalties for exit).

Kihn concludes that his findings support the theory of fund marketing charges in that performance is not the most important determinant of current charges. Services and other marketing-related charges are critical items. Mutual fund companies can learn several lessons from this study: (1) they should pay attention to the tradeoff between front-end loads, 12b1 fees, and deferred charges; (2) customer services are important to investors; and (3) the firm should worry relatively more about image and less about actual financial performance. Investors can also learn several lessons: (1) marketing charges do not add any real value to the fund's financial performance; and (2) they should be better informed about their options.

Chordia, T., 1996, "The Structure of Mutual Fund Charges," *Journal of Financial Economics*, 41, 3-39.

In this paper the author addresses the issues of the diversity of investment strategies and of fees for open-end mutual funds. Chordia explains that mutual funds provide three benefits for investors: (1) they provide diversification; (2) they experience lower transactions costs; and (3) they enable investors to share liquidity risk. He posits that mutual funds seek to dissuade redemptions through load fees and offers a model that funds hold more cash when uncertainty about redemptions increases. The model has several empirical predictions: (1) redemption rates are higher for no-load funds than load funds; (2) closed-end funds are likely to hold less liquid assets; (3) open-end load funds hold assets more liquid than those of closed-end funds; and (4) open-end no-load funds hold the most liquid assets. For purposes of analysis the author employs time-series and cross-sectional data for a total of 397 funds from the period 1984-1993. The results show that rear-load fees are more successful than front-end load fees at lessening redemptions; mutual fund cash holdings decrease with load fees; and that aggressive-growth funds are more likely to rely on load fees for dissuading redemptions because they hold a larger proportion of less liquid stocks. The author concludes that his findings extend readily to other financial intermediaries which must consider the impact of asset redemption on the liquidity of asset holdings.

Malhotra, D. and R. McLeod, 1997, "An Empirical Analysis of Mutual Fund Expenses," *The Journal of Financial Research,* 20, 175-190.

The authors investigate several factors that affect mutual fund expense ratios. The study comprises: (1) an empirical analysis of how ratios differ for a cross-sectional sample of funds, (2) a re-examination of the 12b-1 effect on expenses, and (3) an examination of relative returns for funds with 12b-1 plans. They conduct an analysis of both equity and bond funds with 1,400 fund years of data for the period 1992-1993.

Their model for equity funds includes the following variables: sales charge, size, asset growth, fund objectives, turnover, yield, 12b-1, age, beta, and fund complex size. The model for the expense ratio of bond funds includes: sales charge, average maturity, 12b-1, size, age, beta, asset growth, yield, and fund complex. For stock funds higher expense ratios are positively related to turnover ratios and the existence of 12b-1 plans. Lower expense ratios are positively related to no-load status, fund size, age, and fund complex inclusion. For bond funds, higher sales charges, 12b-1 plans, and higher yields, are associated with high expense ratios. Economies of scale also characterize bond funds. Equity funds with 12b-1 plans earn a lower rate of return than funds without them. In contrast, bond funds with 12b-1 plans perform marginally better than those without them.

Dellva, W. and G. Olson, 1998, "The Relationship Between Mutual Fund Fees and Expenses and Their Effects on Performance," *Financial Review*, 33, 85-103.

The authors address the issue of fees charged by mutual funds: front-end load charges, time-decreasing deferred sale charges, redemption fees upon sale, and 12b-1 fees. They discuss how fees may be justified if they allow lower cost or improved performance for the fund. After briefly describing how expenses and fees have evolved in the industry, they use a sample of 568 mutual funds (1987-1992) to determine if there is any fundamental difference in the various types of fees with respect to expenses and fund performance. They report, among other findings, the following: (1) funds with superior performance usually have lower expense ratios; (2) front-end load funds have lower risk-adjusted performance; (3) 12b-1 plans may be justified and should not necessarily be dismissed; (4) for a given expense ratio redemption fees may be justified; (5) deferred sales charges represent dead-weight cost to investors; and (6) turnover activity raises expenses but does not necessarily increase performance. They conclude that 12b-1 fees, deferred sales charges, and redemption fees on average increase expenses. However, the absence of fees does not indicate superior performance since most funds without fees earn negative risk-adjusted returns.

Huddart, S., 1999, "Reputation and Performance Fee Effects on Portfolio Choice by Investment Advisers," *Journal of Financial Markets,* 2, 227-271.

An investment adviser's compensation consists primarily of "asset fees," as a percentage of net assets under management, and "performance fees," which depend on the realized performance of the portfolio relative to a benchmark. Hence, advisers can increase their income in two ways: (1) by choosing a high-return portfolio, and (2) by convincing investors to purchase additional fund shares.

The author models the interaction among risk-averse investors and advisers in a two-period setting. Most prior work on adviser incentives assumes a one-period model. In the current model investors reallocate their wealth at the end of period one based on their impressions about advisers' abilities. Hence, there is a benefit to advisers in the second period if they appear to be informed at the end of the first period. Attempts to create a good reputation may distort period-one portfolio choices by advisers relative to a single period optimum. The author shows how the reputation effect is influenced by the size of the asset fee and the degree of risk aversion. The paper concludes that imposing a performance fee lessens the distortions caused by reputation concerns of the fund adviser, and improves welfare of the investor.

O'Neal, E., 1999, "Mutual Fund Share Classes and Broker Incentives," *Financial Analysts Journal,* 55, 76-87.

The author discusses the various mutual fund share classes, typically designated A, B, and C, under SEC Rule 18f-3, which represent claims on the same underlying portfolio, but differ in regard to distribution-related expenses. Classes A, B, and C, are characterized by front-end loads, deferred loads, and level loads, respectively.   For investors, deciding among share classes is primarily related to expected holding periods.   However, a broker's compensation on different classes can be calculated as the present value of all commissions, which are a function of transaction size and trading commissions, which are impacted by the growth of net assets. This study documents that these varied broker compensation schemes result in a clear conflict of interest between investors and brokers.

For analysis, the author employs both prospectus information and *Morningstar* data for the 20 largest equity funds as of 1998. Using various growth scenarios and holding periods, the author reports that the present value of broker incentives (commissions) for Class A and Class B shares dominates Class C shares over shorter holding periods.   In contrast, for long holding periods, Class C shares produce greater present values for brokers than do Class A or Class B shares. The author explains that long-term investors should prefer Class A or Class B shares, but that brokers with long-term clients have monetary incentives to sell Class C shares, as is the inverse for short-term investors. The author concludes that an obvious solution to this potentially damaging conflict of interest lies in equivalent broker compensation for all share classes.

Droms, W. and D. Walker, 2001, "Persistence of Mutual Fund Operating Characteristics: Returns, Turnover Rates, and Expense Ratios," *Applied Financial Economics*, 11, 457-466.

The authors discuss prior studies of performance persistence and extend this research with a 20-year data sample in investigating turnover and expense persistence in addition to performance. The basic framework of the tests examines how a particular variable for 1981-1990 is related to the same variable for the prior ten years. Annual mutual fund data for 151 equity funds are used to estimate three models for each of the four persistence variables: total returns,

Jensen risk-adjusted returns, expense ratios, and turnover rates. The authors report that neither returns, expenses, nor turnover, exhibit persistence between the two decades. Also, both asset growth and fund size are not related to investment performance. The authors perform short-term persistence tests for one-, two-, three-, and four-year periods, finding some return persistence for years one through three, but not over four years. The findings for shorter-term persistence appear to be related to the small stock effect, especially during the decade of the 1970s.

PAPERS REVIEWED IN CHRONOLOGICAL ORDER

Herman, E., 1963, "Mutual Fund Management Fee Rates," *The Journal of Finance*, 18, 360-376.

Ferris, S. and D. Chance, 1987, "The Effect of 12b-1 Plans on Mutual Fund Expense Ratios: A Note," *The Journal of Finance,* 42, 1077-1082.

Starks, L., 1987, "Performance Incentive Fees: An Agency Theoretic Approach," *Journal of Financial and Quantitative Analysis*, 22, 17-32.

Chance, D. and S. Ferris, 1991, "Mutual Fund Distribution Fees: An Empirical Analysis of the Impact of Regulation," *The Journal of Financial Services Research,* 5, 25-42.

McLeod, R. and D. Malhotra, 1994, "A Re-examination of the Effect of 12b-1 Plans on Mutual Fund Expense Ratios," *The Journal of Financial Research,* 17, 231-240.

Kihn, J., 1996, "To Load or Not to Load? A Study of Marketing and Distribution Charges of Mutual Funds," *Financial Analysts Journal*, (May/June), 28-36.

Chordia, T., 1996, "The Structure of Mutual Fund Charges," *Journal of Financial Economics,* 41, 3-39.

Malhotra, D. and R. McLeod, 1997, "An Empirical Analysis of Mutual Fund Expenses," *The Journal of Financial Research,* 20, 175-190.

Dellva, W. and G. Olson, 1998, "The Relationship Between Mutual Fund Fees and Expenses and Their Effects on Performance," *Financial Review*, 33, 85-103.

Huddart, S., 1999, "Reputation and Performance Fee Effects on Portfolio Choice by Investment Advisers," *Journal of Financial Markets,* 2, 227-271.

O'Neal, E., 1999, "Mutual Fund Share Classes and Broker Incentives," *Financial Analysts Journal,* 55, 76-87.

Droms, W. and D. Walker, 2001, "Persistence of Mutual Fund Operating Characteristics: Returns, Turnover Rates, and Expense Ratios," *Applied Financial Economics*, 11, 457-466.

4. STYLE ANALYSIS

4.1 Introduction

Sharpe (1992) shows that appropriate "style" classifications enable an investor to effectively diversify. The holdings-based method and the returns-based method are most commonly used to classify funds. Services like *Morningstar* use the holdings-based method, which categorizes funds on the basis of average market capitalization and average price-to-earnings of the fund portfolio. The holdings-based method may be a better way for classifying funds, as historical correlations are poor predictors of future correlations. However, this method requires establishment of boundaries on some differentiating characteristic which is often vague.

Alternately, Trzcinka (1995) and Brown and Goetzman (1997) demonstrate the successful use of the returns-based classification method. Its success is due primarily to the scheme being parsimonious with the data, simple to model, and cost effective in its use. The returns-based method also reduces the management incentive to "game" the styles in order to improve ex-post rankings, and they provide sufficient discrimination between funds, resulting in significant diversification benefits.

Sharpe, W., 1992, "Asset Allocation: Management Style and Performance Management," *Journal of Portfolio Management*, 18, 7-19.

Sharpe explains that asset allocation is usually defined as the allocation of a portfolio across a number of major asset classes and that this construct accounts for a large part of return variability in a typical investor's portfolio. Once a set of asset classes is defined, one can determine the exposure of each component of an investor's portfolio to returns in the respective class. Thus, one can determine how effectively fund managers have performed. Also, the effectiveness of the investor's overall allocation can be compared with benchmark asset mixes. Desirable asset classes should be mutually exclusive, exhaustive, and have differing returns.

In this work the model has 12 asset classes, each of which has returns represented by an appropriate market index. The asset classes range from cash equivalents to long-term government bonds, to value stocks, to Japanese stocks. In determining the investor's exposure to asset classes, the author develops the traditional view of asset allocation, which assumes that the investor's exposure is a function of allocations to various asset class funds. The author explains that "style analysis" consists of employing quadratic programming for determining a fund's exposure to changes in major asset classes' returns and that the goal of style analysis is to infer the fund's exposure to variations in asset class returns during the period of interest. The author performs this procedure for each of 395 funds (1985-1989). For growth-equity funds the most prominent exposure is growth stocks, although these funds also respond to movements in returns of other asset classes. The results illustrate the fact that few funds are pure in their response to the returns of only one asset class. The author then develops how a passive fund manager provides an investor with an investment style, while an active manager provides both style and selection. Sharpe concludes that style analysis can serve as a supplement to other methods in helping investors achieve their investment goals in cost-effective ways.

Grinblatt, M., S. Titman and R. Wermers, 1995, "Momentum Investment Strategies, Portfolio Performance, and Herding: A Study of Mutual Fund Behavior," *American Economic Review,* 85, 1088-1105.

The authors explain the process of mutual funds' using momentum investment strategies, as well as how they exhibit "herding" behavior, which is buying and selling the same stocks at the same time. To examine the trading patterns of fund managers, they analyze the quarterly holdings of 155 mutual funds over the 1975-1984 period. In addition to investigating the extent to which funds purchase stocks based on past returns, and the extent to which they herd, they examine the impact of these behaviors on the performance of the funds. They contrast momentum investors, who buy past winners and sell past losers, with contrarian investors, who do the opposite.

In their analysis the authors employ multiple cross-sectional regressions of fund performance on fund characteristics. They report that about 77% of mutual funds participate in momentum investing and that on average the stocks held by a fund at quarter-end have returns 0.74% higher than the stocks held at the end of the prior quarter. Large-cap past winners contribute almost all of the observed momentum-investing behavior for all fund categories and for the total sample. The results indicate that momentum investors realize higher gross returns than do contrarians, and that both exceed returns from the CRSP index. When the difference in returns between momentum investors and contrarians is risk-adjusted, it is seen that contrarians hold smaller stocks (riskier) than do momentum investors.

When considering herding behavior, the authors show that all funds exhibit more herding in buying past winners than in buying past losers. However, the average measure for all funds is relatively small. They conclude that mutual funds tend to buy stocks based on past returns and that they herd in excess of what one would expect from chance only. The tendency to momentum invest was found to be especially strong, and much more so, than the tendency to herd.

Trzcinka, C., 1995, "Equity Style Classifications: Comment," *The Journal of Portfolio Management,* Spring, 44-46.

The author first briefly explains the three primary approaches used in equity-style clarifications: (1) the portfolio-based approach, which involves an examination of a portfolio and the security selection procedures, (2) the factor model approach using a statistical model which relates excess returns earned for systematic risk, and (3) the "effective mix" approach, which examines the relationship between a portfolio's returns and returns from a passive index strategy. He discusses two points concerning the effective mix model: (1) statistical models employing historical returns are unstable, and (2) returns cannot capture a change in manager style. He summarizes that there are two reasons to question the empirical power of the effective mix: (1) as mentioned above, historical returns produce unstable model parameters, and (2) portfolio-based approaches potentially yield more information. The effective-mix method has an advantage in its simplicity and objectivity, and its best use may be as a form of communication between the money manager and the sponsor.

Gallo, J. and L. Lockwood, 1997, "Benefits of Proper Style Classification of Equity Portfolio Managers," *The Journal of Portfolio Management,* 23, 47-55.

In their discussion of holdings-based versus returns-based methods of style analysis, Gallo and Lockwood explain how the returns-based classification method is simple to model, discriminatory, and cost effective. They also explain how the returns-based method reduces the management incentive to "game" the styles.

Gallo and Lockwood employ 195 equity funds (1978-1993) to create portfolios from each style category and combine them into an equally-weighted portfolio. The authors use a return-based classification scheme wherein the funds are assigned to one of four styles based on their highest loading on Wilshire Style Indexes: large capitalization growth, small capitalization growth, large capitalization value, or small capitalization value. (This contrasts with the conventional classifications of both *Morningstar* and CDA that use manager self-definition and internal assessment, respectively.) The process is repeated 500 times, and the portfolios are held for eight years with quarterly balancing. Sharpe ratios are used to evaluate portfolio performance.

Over the period the equity mutual funds slightly underperform the Wilshire 5000 Index. Also, there are significant differences in the way *Morningstar* and CDA classify the funds. Thus, different classification may lead to different performance within equity style. The authors conclude that their classification scheme provides a "cost effective, objective method that classifies funds and produces significant benefits offered by style diversification."

DiBartolomeo, D. and E. Witkowski, 1997, "Mutual Fund Misclassification: Evidence Based on Style Analysis," *Financial Analysts Journal*, (September/October), 32-43.

In their investigation of mutual fund misclassification, the authors explain that many equity funds exhibit behavior that is inconsistent with what could be expected of funds in their class. The issue of misclassification is important because such classification signals incorrectly, which ultimately allocates assets into less than optimal projects. Misclassification occurs for at least two reasons: (1) the ambiguity of the current classification system, and (2) competitive pressures in the fund industry and compensation structures that reward relative performance.

The authors focus on two questions: (1) Are fund misclassifications random or explainable, and (2) Is misclassification a significant hindrance to investors obtaining their investment objectives? To address these questions, the authors examine the current classification system which was developed by Sharpe (1992). Monthly returns for 748 load and no-load funds are categorized as: aggressive growth, growth, growth-income, income, international, or small capitalization. They examine the relative influence of various investment approaches on each fund with a linear multi-index model and find that 40% of the 748 funds studied ended up in a different category than that declared in their prospectus. For example, of the 93 funds in the small-cap category, 46 were reclassified as aggressive-growth, one as income, and one as growth. To quantify the economic impact of fund misclassification they approximate the total annual wealth generated by the funds that was unexpected, given their class. They report that investors gained approximately one billion dollars because of fund misclassification; however they did so because of additional risk assumed. To control for misclassifications arising from estimation errors, they use Montecarlo-type simulations to create funds for testing. Their findings suggest that the high level of misclassification is not the result of estimation error. Additionally, they employ probit analysis on variables such as fund size, fund company size, manager tenure, fund age, etc. The two variables found to have statistical significance relative to misclassification are membership in a big fund complex (negative impact) and assets in the fund itself (positive impact). They conclude that misclassification is an important problem and that the methodology they present is a way of achieving more accurate peer groupings.

Bogle, J., 1998, "The Implications of Style Analysis for Mutual Fund Performance Evaluation," *The Journal of Portfolio Management,* Summer, 34-42.

Bogel employs the nine-box TIC-TAC-TOE *Morningstar* mutual fund rating system as a discussion point to broach the main focus of his article: the inability of actively managed funds to match the performance of passive investment strategies. He explains that mutual funds' investment styles evolved from being relatively homogeneous during the 1970s to being heterogeneous in recent years. Hence, performance evaluation has changed from using a simple market model to peer-style comparison. The author presents statistics computed by *Morningstar* which show the wide variation in risk-adjusted returns for large, medium, and small funds, respectively. He discusses the impact of expenses on returns and shows that costs are a prime differentiator in the nine-box equity-style analysis. Bogel continues with a discussion of the relative attributes of index mutual funds and compares index fund returns with actively managed equity fund returns. For the period of interest, the average return for all index funds is 15.1%, versus 13.7% for managed funds. Also, the average risk assumed by the actively managed equity funds is far higher: 11.9% for the actively managed group versus 9.7% for the comparably weighted indexes. The final result is that the risk-adjusted ratios average 1.23 for the index funds and 0.99 for the managed funds, which is an average premium of approximately 24% in risk-adjusted return for the five years ending 1996. The author concludes the article by referencing Peter Bernstein's discussion of the market:

> "...if you believe it is efficient (and you are right)... the best strategy is to buy an index fund. If you believe it is efficient (and you are wrong) ... you will

earn the market return, but a few actively
managed funds will beat you. But if you
bet that the market is not efficient, the
probability of underperforming is high.
The risk, in short, is much greater if you
bet on inefficiency rather than on
efficiency."

Fant, L. and E. O'Neal, 1999, "Do You Need More than One
Manager for a Given Equity Style?" *Journal of Portfolio
Management*, 25, 68-76.

The authors address the issue of whether there are any benefits
to diversifying within a mutual fund style category. This work
extends the earlier work of O'Neal (1997) in two ways: (1) they
use style categories rather than fund objective groupings for
classification purposes, and (2) they test for differences in
diversification benefits across style categories. In addressing
alternative measures of risk, the authors develop how a strategy
emphasizing minimal dispersion in terminal wealth levels (TWSD)
is more appropriate than one attempting to reduce short-term return
fluctuations. For analysis, quarterly returns for domestic equity
funds (1992-1996) are used to construct portfolios consisting of 1 –
15 funds in the manner of O'Neal. Simulation results show that all
nine style categories experience reduction in TWSD as the number
of fund managers is increased. Some style categories benefit more
from added managers than do others, with the blend categories
tending to benefit least from diversification, and the growth
categories benefiting most. They conclude that this type of
analysis can be joined with sponsor-specific cost analysis to
determine the optimal number of managers to be employed.

Najand, M. and L. Prather, 1999, "The Risk Level Discriminatory Power of Mutual Fund Investment Objectives: Additional Evidence," *Journal of Financial Markets,* 2, 307-328.

The authors reexamine the information content of mutual fund investment objectives to determine their validity as a tool for inferring investor risk. A brief review of earlier studies discusses that investment objectives are useful in conveying risk. However, more recently, Brown, Harlow, and Starks (1996) report that fund managers often manipulate risk for various reasons.

For investment objectives to realistically convey risk, they should be: (1) systematically related to a measure of risk such as beta or volatility, (2) homogeneous within investment objective category, and (3) heterogeneous between categories. If investment objectives properly convey risk, comparing funds within a category is proper, but improper otherwise. If information asymmetry about fund risk and imperfect monitoring both exist, problems may arise. Portfolio managers who believe that investors will view only returns and disregard risk differences may accept additional risk to increase returns in order to create the appearance of superior performance.

The authors employ a sample of 377 funds (9/81 – 9/94) and sort these funds by eight CDA investment objectives. Systematic risk is computed, and they find that five of the eight investment objective categories have heterogeneous within-group risk significant at the 0.01 level. Thus, it appears that CDA classification misses some important characteristic of risk or that managers manipulate risk. They conclude that this within-group risk heterogeneity may result from competition in the fund industry, imperfect monitoring by regulators and investors, and/or portfolio manager compensation schemes.

Gallo, J. and L. Lockwood, 1999, "Fund Management Changes and Equity Style Shifts," *The Journal of Portfolio Management,* 55, 44-52.

This paper studies the performance of a fund when it shifts from one style to another. Performance is analyzed using traditional measures such as the Sharpe ratio and Jensen's alpha. In addition, the authors investigate managerial capabilities such as security selection and market timing by using the Treynor-Mazuy models. Equity styles are constructed by classifying a mutual fund into one of four style categories based on the sensitivity of a fund's standardized returns to those of the four Wilshire indices: large capitalization growth (LCG), small capitalization growth (SCG), large capitalization value (LCV) and small capitalization value (SCV). In equation (1) regression coefficients (betas) are the sensitivities of the standardized returns of a fund on the standardized returns of the Wilshire indices. A fund is classified into the category of its highest beta weight using the following:

$$R_{it} = b_{i0} + b_{i1}R_{LCG,t} + b_{i2}R_{SCG,t} + b_{i3}R_{LCV,t} + b_{i4}R_{SCV,t} + \varepsilon_{it}. \quad (1)$$

Results indicate that performance is generally below the benchmark prior to management change and then match the benchmark after the change. Security selection ability is significantly improved after a management change. The average change in the market timing coefficient is statistically indifferent between pre- and post-management changes. Thus, performance on average improves after management changes.

PAPERS REVIEWED IN CHRONOLOGICAL ORDER

Sharpe, W., 1992, "Asset Allocation: Management Style and Performance Management," *Journal of Portfolio Management*, 18, 7-19.

Grinblatt, M., S. Titman and R. Wermers, 1995, "Momentum Investment Strategies, Portfolio Performance, and Herding: A Study of Mutual Fund Behavior," *American Economic Review,* 85, 1088-1105.

Trzcinka, C., 1995, "Equity Style Classifications: Comment," *The Journal of Portfolio Management, Spring*, 44-46.

Gallo, J. and L. Lockwood, 1997, "Benefits of Proper Style Classification of Equity Portfolio Managers," *The Journal of Portfolio Management*, 23, 47-55.

DiBartolomeo, D. and E. Witkowski, 1997, "Mutual Fund Misclassification: Evidence Based on Style Analysis," *Financial Analysts Journal*, (September/October), 32-43.

Brown, S. and W. Goetzmann, 1997, "Mutual Fund Styles," *Journal of Financial Economics*, 43, 373-399.

Bogle, J., 1998, "The Implications of Style Analysis for Mutual Fund Performance Evaluation," *The Journal of Portfolio Management,* Summer, 34-42.

Fant, L. and E. O'Neal, 1999, "Do You Need More Than One Manager for a Given Equity Style? Evidence from Mutual Funds," *The Journal of Portfolio Management,* Summer, 68-75.

Najand, M. and L. Prather, 1999, "The Risk Level Discriminatory Power of Mutual Fund Investment Objectives: Additional Evidence," *Journal of Financial Markets,* 2, 307-328.

Gallo, J. and L. Lockwood, 1999, "Fund Management Changes and Equity Style Shifts," *The Journal of Portfolio Management,* 55, 44-52.

5. FUND FLOWS

5.1 Introduction

Studies addressing fund flows focus on a wide variety of topics, ranging from investors' reactions to fund performance, to the impact of market movements on flows, to the effect of fund flows on market level changes. In an early fund flow study, Smith (1978) finds support that shows that improved fund performance attracts new money to funds. In a related vein, Ippolito (1992) reports that over time poor-quality funds lose market share to high-quality funds. The issue of why these poorly-performing funds continue to exist is addressed by Harless and Peterson (1998). Related works involve issues ranging from Edelen's (1999) analysis of the impact of flows on performance to the impact of fund advertising on flows.

Smith, K., 1978, "Is Fund Growth Related to Fund Performance?" *The Journal of Portfolio Management,* 5, 49-54.

This article was inspired by the question, "What causes an individual to select one mutual fund over another?" Smith focuses on the relationship between fund growth and performance of funds over time. To address the issue he proposes two hypotheses:

> Growth Hypothesis: Mutual funds that improve their performance in a given period experience a growth rate in assets under management during the next period that is no different from that of mutual funds that did not improve their performance.

> New Money Hypothesis: Mutual funds that
> improve their performance in a given period
> experience a growth rate in outstanding shares
> during the next period that is no different from
> that of mutual funds that did not improve their
> performance.

He uses a sample of 74 funds (1966-1975) and employs both growth and risk-adjusted performance. For the growth hypothesis the risk-adjusted returns are more strongly associated with growth than with the *Forbes* ratings (gross). For the new money hypothesis he reports that risk-adjusted performance improvement leads to an above-average increase in mutual fund shares outstanding, thus providing support that new money is attracted to funds exhibiting improved performance. He calls for further research to understand the total relationship between fund performance and growth.

Ippolito, R., 1992, "Consumer Reaction to Measures of Poor Quality: Evidence from the Mutual Fund Industry," *Journal of Law and Economics,* 35, 45-70.

The author notes that the market for mutual funds delivers high-quality products over long periods and explores the hypothesis that fund investor vigilance plays a significant role in generating an efficient equilibrium in this market. He explains that funds use the fees and expenses assessed beyond similar index fund charges to seek out and act on information to benefit shareholders. Thus, investors expect net risk-adjusted returns at least equal to those of index funds. A high-quality fund is defined as one that adds value to off-set incremental expenses. A low-quality fund assesses similar expenses, but generates systematically lower returns. The author's model presents mutual fund investors who evaluate quality by observing recent risk-adjusted performance. Ippolito explains that transactions costs affect investors' decisions to react to fund performance, and that costs explain the relatively smooth movement of monies among investor accounts; thus over time poor-quality funds lose market share to high-quality funds.

A sample of 143 funds over the period 1965-1984 is analyzed initially using a pooled regression and a fixed effects model. It is found that funds that outperform the market experience a stronger response in growth rate than do poorly performing funds. Also, investors respond more strongly to performance in actively managed funds and in capital appreciation funds than in other types of funds. The author concludes that the data reveal a clear movement of monies toward recent good performers and away from poor performers. In a policy context the author states that the mutual fund industry provides an observation in favor of an information approach to regulation.

Warther, V., 1997, "Aggregate Mutual Fund Flows and Security Returns," *Journal of Financial Economics,* 39, 209-235.

This study investigates fund flows and returns at the macro level. It contrasts with earlier papers that study the relationship between individual fund performance and money in-flows at the micro level. There are two primary questions addressed: (1) Are total in-flows associated with concurrent or subsequent market movements? and (2) Are mutual fund investors feedback-traders who invest in response to market movements? Tangential questions considered involve small-stock returns and closed-end fund discounts.

Using monthly and weekly data, the author divides fund-flows into anticipated and unanticipated flows, in addition to tracking net flows of money into different mutual fund sectors. The study finds that flows into stock funds and bond funds are strongly correlated; whereas stock fund and money market flows are negatively

correlated. Unexpected net flows into funds are correlated with
concurrent security returns, but expected flows are uncorrelated with
concurrent returns. Flows into stock funds, bond funds, and precious
metal funds are correlated with returns from their respective sectors.
There is no positive relation between flows and lagged returns;
hence, feedback trading by mutual fund investors has little support.
Neither proxy for investor sentiment, small stock behavior, or closed-
end fund discount behavior, is strongly associated with fund flows.

Lettau M., 1997, "Explaining the Facts with Adaptive Agents: The
Case of Mutual Fund Flows," *Journal of Economic Dynamics and
Control,* 21, 1117-1147.

The author studies portfolio decisions of boundedly rational
agents in a financial market. The primary focus of the work is on
how investors change holdings between mutual funds with different
risky investments. Agents must decide how much to invest in a
single risky asset, and they learn from outcomes of past investment
decisions. Learning takes place over a one-period investment
horizon as repeated one-shot investment decisions. Two versions of
the model are utilized: one models a population of agents whose
portfolio converges to a single value over the agents' lifetime; and
the other consists of a population of agents with new entries and
exits. This allows the author to compare the behavior of adaptive
agents to fund flow data.

Via a series of simulations, the author finds that the adaptive
agents tend to hold too much of the risky asset owing to more
positive than negative events. Lettau also empirically investigates
flows into and out of mutual funds using monthly data from
February 1985 through December 1992. The data set focuses on
aggregate flows of different fund categories: aggressive growth,
growth and income, growth, and balanced portfolios. Investors
change their portfolio composition after observing market outcomes

and tend to react more to negative market outcomes than to positive ones. The author concludes that investors in funds show the same investment patterns as the adaptive agents in the model presented, as contrasted with standard theories having rational agents.

Santini, D. and J. Aber, 1998, "Determinants of Net New Money Flows to the Equity Mutual Fund Industry," *Journal of Economics and Business,* 50, 419-429.

Santini and Aber briefly review the findings of earlier works which investigate aggregate fund flows relative to expense ratios, load status, and a host of other variables. They extend Warther's (1995) analysis by investigating the relationship of fund flows and several variables: interest rate levels, additional measures of risk-adjusted and non-risk-adjusted performance, and changes in personal disposable income. They address three questions: (1) Can they confirm an increase in explanatory power at the aggregate level as opposed to the individual fund level? (2) Can they better determine which factors might be related to fund flows? and (3) Can they confirm Warther's finding of no support for the feedback-trader hypothesis?

In their analysis of 127 funds (1973-1985) the authors define new flows as additional net investment exclusive of reinvested dividends and capital gains, as well as net redemptions. They employ a series of regressions with both contemporaneous and lagged performance and income variables. Results show that new money flows are negatively related to real long-term interest rates and positively related to personal income and stock market performance. Their lagged performance results, as employed by Warther, lack statistical significance; thereby they reject the feedback-trader hypothesis.

Harless, D. and S. Peterson, 1998, "Investor Behavior and the Persistence of Poorly-performing Mutual Funds," *Journal of Economic Behavior and Organization,* 37, 257-276.

This article addresses the issue of how investor behavior allows consistently poorly-performing funds to continue in existence. For example, the 44 Wall Street Fund reported an annual − 7.4% risk-adjusted return for the years 1974-1988, but continued to exist. This occurrence appears to contradict Ippolito's (1992) claim that investor behavior keeps the mutual fund industry efficient.

The authors compare two models for testing the flow of assets to funds: (1) investor holdings in mutual funds are determined on the basis of past risk-adjusted returns and are subject to a partial-adjustment process, and (2) investor behavior may be explained by the representativeness heuristic. Such a heuristic indicates three ways that investors can deviate from evaluating funds on a risk-adjusted basis: (1) inappropriately adjusting for systematic risk, (2) ignoring expense ratios' predictive validity, or (3) focusing primarily on most recent return. Using a sample of 100 funds (1977-1992), they find that investors do not employ returns and risk in accordance with a Jensen's alpha prescription. Instead, judgments about fund performance are biased by extreme recent gross returns, and judgments also ignore the predictive validity of expense differences for long-run performance, thus allowing poorly performing funds to survive.

Sirri, E., and P. Tufano, 1998, "Costly Search and Mutual Fund Flows," *The Journal of Finance,* 53, 1589-1622.

In the first half of this paper the authors perform an analysis of mutual fund flows utilizing nearly two decades of data (1972-1990), which includes 690 funds offered by 288 different fund families. This is followed by an analysis of costly search for fund flows.

Assuming that consumers obtain fund information at zero cost, one might expect to find: (1) a performance-flow relationship among the worst-performing funds, (2) a possibly weaker, but observable performance-flow among the best performance funds, (3) a negative relationship between risk and flows, and (4) a negative relationship between fees charged and flows. The relationship between relative returns and flows is discussed insofar as performance is associated with inflows. Findings indicate that consumers seem to prefer funds with less risk and lower fees. In addition to gross returns and risk measures, alternative performance specifications are employed, yielding similar findings. To address survivorship bias the authors examine data from 1987-1990, when virtually all data are available. They continue to find strong performance sensitivity among high performers and a weaker relationship among poor performers.

The second half of the paper addresses the issue of search costs. They employ three related proxies for product identification costs: mutual fund complex size, marketing and distribution expenditures, and media coverage. They report that funds in larger complexes do not necessarily enjoy a stronger performance-flow relationship. Reductions in expense ratios are most strongly related to fund flows, with annual fee reductions positively affecting flows. However, there appears to be little differential performance-flow response between more and less media attention.

Edwards, F. and X. Zhang, 1998, "Mutual Funds and Stock and Bond Market Stability," *The Journal of Financial Services Research*, 13, 257-282.

This paper addresses the relationships between fund flows and stock and bond prices. Specifically, the authors analyze the relationship between aggregate monthly flows into both stock and bond funds and monthly equity and bond prices by employing different causal economic procedures. For purposes of analysis, equity fund flows and bond fund flows are examined for the periods 1961-1996 and 1976-1996, respectively. Two statistical procedures are employed: (1) Granger causality analysis is employed to examine the "lead-lag" relationships between the two variables of interest, and (2) an instrumental variables procedure is utilized to examine additional economic factors affecting flows and asset returns.

The Granger causality tests indicate that fund sales have an effect on asset returns. In contrast, Granger tests strongly support the conclusion that fund sales are impacted by asset returns. The instrumental variables analysis yields similar but more robust results, thereby strengthening the findings of the Granger analysis. The authors conclude that the run-up in stock prices prior to 1996 is not attributable to the growth of equity funds during the 1980s and 1990s. Also, results indicate that the possibility of downward pressure on stock prices induced by fund sales during the 1971-1981 period cannot be dismissed.

Zheng, L., 1999, "Is Money Smart? A Study of Mutual Fund Investors' Fund Selection Ability," *The Journal of Finance,* 54, 632-665.

The author states that most of the earlier studies of fund performance address the investment performance of mutual fund managers. Previously, only Gruber (1996) addresses the ability of investors to select funds. He reports that the return on new cash flows into funds exceeds the average return for all investors in these funds. In a similar vein Zheng examines the statistical and economic significance of two effects:

- *Gruber's "smart money" effect*: Whether investors are smart ex ante, as they move to funds that will perform better.

- *The information effect*: Whether investors' moves yield information that can be used to generate abnormal returns.

Using a sample of all equity funds (1970-1993), the author applies a performance test (Grinblatt and Titman, 1993) to examine the smart money effect. Secondly, different trading strategies are used to investigate both the smart money effect and the information effect. For the strategies, eight different methods, each based on newly invested money signals, are employed. Two aggregate methods are used to calculate risk-adjusted returns of each portfolio: (1) a portfolio regression approach, and (2) both a one-factor and three-factor time-series regression. Following several analyses the author reports that the trading strategies confirm that newly-invested money in funds forecasts short-term future fund performance. However, investors cannot beat the market by investing in funds with positive new money flow. A possible exception is that the positive new money flow of small funds outperforms the market. The smart money effect is short-lived, as the performance rankings of the positive and negative portfolios reverse after 30 months. The author concludes that the smart money effect is not due to a style effect or macroeconomic information, but is likely due to fund-specific information.

Edelen, R., 1999, "Investor Flows and the Assessed Performance of Open-end Mutual Funds," *Journal of Financial Economics,* 53, 439-466.

In this article the author explains that conventional mutual fund performance analysis gives no weight to the fact that managers provide liquidity, as a result of fund flows, to investors and in doing so engage in material liquidity-motivated trading. The providing of a liquid equity position to investors can result in negative abnormal returns for informed fund managers. Therefore, performance measures that do not account for flow-induced trading can yield negatively biased inferences concerning a manager's ability to choose mispriced securities. He also explains that prior studies of market-timing performance suffer the same fault. This work extends earlier market timing findings by revealing the effectiveness of using the fund's flows as a conditioning variable.

The author develops that a fund's alpha should be composed of: (1) a positive term for the manager's information trading, and (2) a negative term related to the fund's realized flow. In considering market timing performance, if flow is positively correlated with the frequently observed one-day return autocorrelations, then flow may give rise to negative market timing owing to subsequent market returns. For analysis the author employs 166 mutual funds for the period 1985-90. The data reveal that one-half of the average fund's assets are redeemed in the course of one year, and the average annualized rate of turnover is 90% of fund assets.

Employing both time-series regressions and cross-sectional regressions, the author finds that expenses and brokerage commissions each contribute roughly 30 basis points to the liquidity trading effect. Also, the costs associated with providing liquidity are a function of trading activity in general. In the absence of liquidity demands, the average abnormal return is not significantly different from zero. Thus, although average fund performance is -1.63% annually, following the conventional approach to performance evaluation, there is no underperformance when a liquidity-adjusted benchmark is applied. In addressing the market timing test, the author employs the procedure used by Traynor and Mazury (1966) and finds that the appearance of negative market timing performance is due to the liquidity service effect. He concludes that funds' underperformance has little to do with fund manager ability, but rather results from the liquidity service provided by managers.

Fant, L., 1999, "Investment Behavior of Mutual Fund Shareholders: The Evidence from Aggregate Fund Flows," *The Journal of Financial Markets,* 2, 391-402.

Fant examines the relationship between fund flows and stock market returns. Aggregate fund flows are broken down into four components: (1) new sales, (2) redemptions, (3) exchanges-in (transfers within a fund complex), and (4) exchanges-out (again, transfers). The author explains that investors can more easily move funds via exchanges than sales or redemptions. Aggregate fund flows for the period 1984-95 are used in vector autoregressions to analyze the dependence between returns and flow components, as well as between the components themselves. The study reports that there is no relationship between returns and new sales or redemptions. Returns are positively related to exchanges-in, and negatively related to exchanges-out. There is also a common variation between sales/redemptions and exchanges-in/out that is unrelated to stock returns. New sales and redemptions are more predictable than exchanges-in/out. These findings indicate that fund investors use new sales/redemptions differently from exchanges. Investors appear to use exchanges when attempting to time the market. In contrast, new sales/redemptions appear to reflect long-term risk premia. The author concludes that further research in the flow-return relationship should focus on exchanges-in/out.

Jain, P. and J. Wu, 2000, "Truth in Mutual Fund Advertising: Evidence on Future Performance and Fund Flows," *The Journal of Finance,* 55, 937-958.

The authors' two main objectives are: (1) to test whether mutual fund advertisements signal superior management skills, and (2) to test whether advertising attracts more money to the mutual funds. They briefly discuss SEC fund advertising guidelines, which require funds to report one-, five-, and ten-year performance (if extant for that period). The reporting time period must be at least one-year long ending with the latest calendar quarter.

Using a sample of 294 open-end funds advertised in *Barron's* or *Money* from 7/18/94 through 6/30/96, they employ four benchmarks for analysis: (1) average return for like investment objective funds, (2) return on the S&P 500 Index, (3) Jensen's one-factor alpha, and (4) a four-factor alpha described in Carhart (1997). The four-factor model is described as follows:

$$R_{it} - R_{ft} = \alpha_i + \beta_{1i}(R_{mt} - R_{ft}) + \beta_{2i}SMB_t + \beta_{2i}HML_t \\ + \beta_{2i}Momentum + \varepsilon_t \tag{1}$$

where SMB = small- minus large-cap portfolio returns, HML = high- minus low-book-to-market stock portfolio returns, and Momentum = high- minus low-momentum stock portfolio returns.

Table 5.1 – Performance of Funds Pre- and Post-Advertisement			
	Raw Returns	Similar Fund Adjusted Return	4-Factor Alpha
Pre-advertisement Period			
All Funds (N=294)	25.55	5.98 (11.15*)	1.43 (2.44*)
Unique Funds (N=117)	22.92	6.26 (8.31*)	2.06 (2.62*)
Post-advertisement Period			
All Funds (N=294)	18.52	-0.82 (-1.38)	-3.45 (-6.08*)
Unique Funds (N=117)	19.48	-0.37 (-0.35)	-3.56 (-3.81*)

* Significant at 5%

Results show that funds' pre-advertisement period returns outperform their benchmarks. However, results for these funds in the post-advertisement period show no persistence in superior performance and even some evidence of performance reversal (see Table 5.1). In further analysis the authors examine whether advertisements yield higher money flows to the advertised funds and find that money inflows are approximately 20% greater than for the control group.

PAPERS REVIEWED IN CHRONOLOGICAL ORDER

Smith, K., 1978, "Is Fund Growth Related to Fund Performance?" *The Journal of Portfolio Management,* 5, 49-54.

Ippolito, R., 1992, "Consumer Reaction to measures of Poor Quality: Evidence from the Mutual Fund Industry," *Journal of Law and Economics,* 35, 45-70.

Warther, V., 1997, "Aggregate Mutual Fund Flows and Security Returns," *Journal of Financial Economics,* 39, 209-235.

Lettau M., 1997, "Explaining the Facts with Adaptive Agents: The Case of Mutual Fund Flows," *Journal of Economic Dynamics and Control,* 21, 1117-1147.

Santini, D. and J. Aber, 1998, "Determinants of Net New Money Flows to the Equity Mutual Fund Industry," *Journal of Economics and Business,* 50, 419-429.

Harless, D. and S. Peterson, 1998, "Investor Behavior and the Persistence of Poorly-performing Mutual Funds," *Journal of Economic Behavior and Organization,* 37, 257-276.

Sirri, E., and P. Tufano, 1998, "Costly Search and Mutual Fund Flows," *The Journal of Finance,* 53, 1589-1622.

Edwards, F. and X. Zhang, 1998, "Mutual Funds and Stock and Bond Market Stability," *The Journal of Financial Services Research,* 13, 257-282.

Zheng, L., 1999, "Is Money Smart? A Study of Mutual Fund Investors' Fund Selection Ability," *The Journal of Finance,* 54, 632-665.

Edelen, R., 1999, "Investor Flows and the Assessed Performance of Open-end Mutual Funds," *Journal of Financial Economics,* 53, 439-466.

Fant, L., 1999, "Investment Behavior of Mutual Fund Shareholders: The Evidence from Aggregate Fund Flows," *The Journal of Financial Markets,* 2, 391-402.

Jain, P. and J. Wu, 2000, "Truth in Mutual Fund Advertising: Evidence on Future Performance and Fund Flows," *The Journal of Finance,* 55, 937-958.

6. SPECIALTY FUNDS

6.1 Introduction

In this chapter we present summaries of several of the more frequently cited works addressing mutual funds which do not fit into the various categories of equity funds. Fund types included are: hedge funds, international funds, bond funds, and socially responsible funds. Before proceeding to the summaries, we briefly discuss some characteristics of these specialty funds.

Hedge funds-- These funds have been around for half a century and have grown at the rate of 25% per year for the past two decades. The funds are typically investment partnerships with fewer than 100 investors, which allows them to be exempt from the Investment Company Act of 1940. Hedge funds are typically stratified by trading strategies and asset type. Managed Report Accounts, Inc. lists the following major categories: Event Driven (Distressed Securities, Risk Arbitrage), Global (International, Emerging, or Regional), Global Macro, Market Neutral (Long/Short, Convertible Arbitrage, Stock Index Arbitrage, Fixed Income Arbitrage), Short Sales, U.S. Opportunistic (Growth, Value), Fund of Funds.

International Funds-- International diversification can produce significant reductions in systematic risk, and many U.S. investors diversify internationally by using mutual funds. At the end of 1984, 37 international equity mutual funds with assets of approximately $6 billion traded in the U.S. By the late 1990s the number of funds was approximately 130 with assets of $280 billion.

Bond funds— Returns to bond funds are primarily driven by interest rate changes. These funds are expected to exhibit management consistency because of their relative homogeneity. In

1978 bond funds held only 10% of the total net assets of mutual funds, compared to approximately 22% today.

Socially Responsible Funds-- Corporate social policy has become an important informational issue to many investors over the past decade, and many socially responsible investors favor certain companies over others according to their own socio-political beliefs. These investors define corporate goals more broadly than the traditional textbook ideal of shareholder wealth maximization and are motivated by concern over their firms' actions in areas such as equal employment opportunity, product safety, environmental health, and workplace policies.

6.2 Hedge Funds

Brown, S., W. Goetzmann, and R. Ibbotson, 1999, "Offshore Hedge Funds: Survival and Performance, 1989-95," *The Journal of Business*, 72, 91-117.

The authors explain that hedge funds are somewhat similar to mutual funds in structure and diversification, but that they differ dramatically in many respects. For instance, they may sell short, use leverage, and employ derivatives. Many view these funds as being market-neutral "bets" on managers who seek out and exploit mispriced financial assets using a variety of financial instruments and strategies. Of particular interest in this article are offshore hedge funds, which differ from domestic vehicles in that they are usually incorporated in tax havens such as the Bahamas or British Virgin Islands. The article examines the performance of the universe of offshore hedge funds over the period 1989 to 1995.

Table 6.1 shows the annual summary statistics for the universe of offshore hedge funds. Table 6.2 shows the fund performance by style category.

		Table 6.1 – Offshore Hedge Fund Annual Statistics			
Year	Number of Funds	Total Market Cap ($ billions)	Median Return	Average Annual Fee	Incentive Fee
1988-89	78	4.72	20.30	1.744	19.755
1989-90	108	6.15	3.80	1.647	19.519
1990-91	142	11.46	15.90	1.786	19.548
1991-92	176	18.87	1070	1.809	19.344
1992-93	265	39.06	22.15	1.621	19.096
1993-94	313	35.41	-2.00	1.644	18.753
1994-95	399	40.34	14.70	1.551	18.497

	Table 6.2 – Offshore Hedge Fund Performance Statistics				
Style	Mean (%)	SD (%)	Alpha (%)	Beta	Sharpe Ratio
Multi	18.48	19.81	7.9	0.471	0.637
Event Driven	14.41	22.15	5.0	0.364	0.387
Market Model	9.87	11.80	4.9	-0.035	0.356
Market Timing	22.07	16.91	12.1	0.413	0.956
U.S. Opportunity	16.48	12.73	4.0	0.644	0.907
Sector	25.73	21.46	8.2	1.092	0.958
Global	33.04	21.85	24.5	0.285	1.236
Fund of Funds	16.95	14.44	6.4	0.464	0.766
Short Sellers	-11.08	19.41	-2.8	-0.960	-0.767
Derivatives	15.36	6.16	7.2	0.249	1.376

The authors report that hedge fund returns have little correlation with U.S. market returns, although there is evidence of positive risk-adjusted returns over time. They conclude that there is little evidence of differential manager skill over time.

Ackermann, C., R. McEnally, and D. Ravenscraft, 1999, "The Performance of Hedge Funds: Risk, Return and Incentives," *The Journal of Finance*, 54, 833-874.

This paper expands the hedge fund literature in four directions: (1) using a larger data set that includes both U.S. and offshore funds, (2) performing data-conditioning bias analyses, (3) potentially explaining the superior performance of these funds, and (4) exploring the determinants of fund risk. The authors discuss several fund characteristics that may influence performance: investment strategies, managerial incentives, managerial investment, client sophistication, and limited government oversight.

Data for 906 funds (1988-1995) from Managed Report Accounts are used for analysis. Table 6.3 shows statistics for hedge funds as of December 31, 1995.

Table 6.3 – Hedge Fund Characteristics			
Feature	Mean	Median	Standard Deviation
Annual Mngt. Fee (%)	1.25	1	0.65
Incentive Fee (%)	13.8	20	9.2
Size ($ millions)	108	27	320
Age (months)	62	49	42
U.S. vs. Offshore	0.52	1	0.50

Results for hedge funds average between 9.2% and 16.1% annually over an eight-year observation period. Event Driven and U.S. Opportunistic funds outperform all other classes during more recent years, although Global and Global Macro funds are the most successful over the longer period. Hedge fund returns match their benchmarks, such as the S&P 500 Index or the Morgan Stanley

International Index. Any ability to outperform the market depends upon the time period, the type of benchmark, and the category of hedge fund. Overall, hedge funds earn returns sufficient to offset the cost of running them. However, they outperform other mutual funds on a risk-adjusted basis.

Of the several variables considered, incentive fee is the most significant in explaining the risk-adjusted performance of hedge funds. Having an incentive fee improves the Sharpe ratio by an average of 66%. Table 6.4 summarizes the annualized returns.

Table 6.4 – Hedge Fund Performance				
MAR Category	Sample Period (in years)	Mean (%)	Mean Relative to S&P 500 (%)	Mean Relative to MSCI EAFE (%)
Total	2	9.2	-10.3	-0.6
	8	16.1	-0.4	7.5
Event Driven	2	11.1	-8.3	1.3
	8	17.9	1.4	9.2
Fund of Funds	2	3.2	-16.3	-6.6
	8	11.4	-5.1	2.8
Global	2	5.7	-13.7	-4.1
	8	19.3	2.7	10.6
Global Macro	2	9.8	-9.6	0.0
	8	19.5	4.0	11.8
Market Neutral	2	9.9	-9.6	0.1
	8	8.0	-8.6	-0.7
Short Sales	2	5.6	-13.8	-4.2
	8	n/a	n/a	n/a
U.S. Opportunistic	2	16.0	-3.4	6.3
	8	14.9	-1.7	6.2

Liang, B., 1999, "On the Performance of Hedge Funds," *Financial Analysts Journal,* 55, 72-85.

Laing explains that hedge funds provide managers with a more competitive fee structure and that incentive fees are paid only when the fund crosses a certain hurdle rate. A majority of funds also have a "high watermark" provision, under which a manger has to make up any previous loses before an incentive clause kicks in. Unlike mutual funds, which are judged relative to some benchmark, hedge funds are judged for their absolute performance.

Using data for 385 hedge funds and for 4,776 mutual funds (1992-1996), the author reports the following averages for hedge funds: assets of $93 million, management fees of 1.36%, incentive fees of 16.24%, and a minimum lock-up period of 84 days. The author employs an asset-class factor model which uses eight asset classes ranging from U.S. equities (S&P 500) to commodities (gold). The factor model is:

$$R_t = \alpha + \sum_{k=1}^{8} \beta_k F_{k,t} + \varepsilon_t , \qquad (1)$$

where R_t is the average fund return in month t; α is the unexplained return by asset class factor; β_k is the factor loading, and F_{kt} is the value of the kth asset class factor. A regression is run on a sample stratified by trading strategy such as convertible arbitrage, market neutral, short selling, and market timing. Results indicate that hedge funds follow dynamic trading strategies and that no one asset class dominates. Eleven of 16 groups have a positive alpha, with only two groups having significant negative αlpha.

To further examine the determinants of hedge fund returns Liang regresses fund returns on fund characteristics such as incentive fees, management fees, lockup period, age, and fund assets. Results show that incentive fees and longer lockups, but not management fees, are associated with high performance.

Finally, the average hedge fund outperforms the average mutual funds, as seen in higher Sharpe ratios. Hedge funds also have lower market beta, but higher total risk, possibly attributable to the use of derivatives and leverage. Liang concludes that the performance superiority of hedge funds is a function of effective incentive schemes, dynamic and flexible trading strategies, and the use of a large variety of financial instruments.

Liang, B., 2001, "Hedge Fund Performance: 1990-1999," *Financial Analysts Journal,* 57, 11-19.

This study updates the results from Liang (1999). The author discusses that several prominent hedge funds faced problems and that one fund, Long Term Capital Management, failed following the 1997 Asian financial crisis. Despite these events and the spectacular bail-out orchestrated by the Federal Reserve, the public has little understanding of these funds. This is partially due to the fact that information on returns, risk, and fee structures are largely unavailable to the public because many hedge funds are non-regulated U.S. partnerships or offshore corporations.

The data for this study spans the ten-year period between 1990 and 1999 and includes 1,407 live and 609 dead funds. The average annual return for the hedge funds is 14.2%, compared to the average annualized S&P 500 return of 18.8%. Among style types the winners are the opportunities and long-bias strategies, and the losers are the systematic and technical strategies. Although the S&P 500 outperforms the hedge funds, this performance comes at the cost of higher risk. On a risk-adjusted basis the entire sample of funds, both surviving and defunct, outperforms the S&P 500.

6.3 International Funds

Cumby, R. and J. Glen, 1990, "Evaluating the Performance of International Mutual Funds," *The Journal of Finance*, 45, 497-521.

This paper, among the earliest international fund works, evaluates the performance of 15 international equity funds spanning the period of 1982 to 1988. Abnormal performance is measured using both Jensen's alpha and Grinblatt and Titman's positive period weighting measure. Two benchmark portfolios are employed: (1) the Morgan Stanley World Index, and (2) a two-benchmark portfolio comprising the world index and an equally weighted portfolio of Eurocurrency deposits.

Jensen measures using the Morgan Stanley World Index for the 15 funds are mostly negative. Only three of the 15 funds report a positive Jensen measure, but none is statistically significant. Tests do not reject the null hypothesis that Jensen measures are statistically different from zero. Using a two-portfolio benchmark (World Index and Eurocurrency deposits), Jensen measures are again negative with no instance of significant superior performance. The positive period weighting measures are remarkably similar to the Jensen measures, both in magnitude and statistical significance. The authors conclude that international fund returns do not surpass those of international indices over this period.

Gallo, J. and P. Swanson, 1996 "Comparative Measures of Performance for U.S.-Based International Equity Mutual Funds," *Journal of Banking and Finance*, 20, 1635-1650.

Gallo and Swanson analyze 37 funds spanning a nine-year period 1985-1993. Tests are run on each of the 37 funds plus on an equally weighted portfolio of the funds, thereby mitigating some of the problems with cross-correlation and heteroscedasticity in fund returns.

Three models are used to detect abnormal performance: (1) Sharpe ratio, (2) alpha using an international 2-index model, and (3) alpha using the International Arbitrage Pricing Theory (IAPT) model. The international index model assumes the following return-generating function:

$$R_{it} = \alpha_i + \beta_{i1}R_{wt} + \beta_{i2}R_{xt} + \varepsilon_{it} ,$$

(1)

where: R_{it} is the excess monthly return for the international mutual funds, R_{wt} is the excess monthly in the Morgan Stanley World Index, and R_{xt} is the excess monthly return on the X131 Dollar Index. Abnormal return using the IAPT is constructed as:

$$R_{it} = \hat{\alpha}_i + b_{i1}f_{1t} + b_{i2}f_{2t} + e_{it}$$

(2)

where α_i and $\hat{\alpha}_i$ indicates superior (inferior) investment performance for fund i. Results show that 15 international mutual funds outperform MSCI, but the Sharpe ratio for the portfolio of funds is equal to that of MSCI. Thus, as measured by total risk, international funds on average match the MSCI market proxy.

The α_i and $\hat{\alpha}_i$ from the index and IAPT model produce conflicting results. The portfolio of funds yields a statistically insignificant positive Jensen measure, but the Jensen measure from the IAPT is positive and statistically significant. The IAPT also has higher explanatory power than the two-index international model in equation (1).

Kao, G., L. Cheng, and K. Chan, 1998, "International Mutual Fund Selectivity and Market Timing During Up and Down Market Conditions," *The Financial Review*, 33, 127-144

This study examines the securities selection and market timing abilities of U.S.-based international fund managers. The study posits that fund managers with superior timing ability should be able to predict broad market movements, and to adjust their portfolios accordingly. During up markets the fund managers are likely to shift their asset allocation towards high-risk securities, while switching to low risk securities during down markets. Thus, the systematic risk of the portfolios does not stay constant over time. To account for this non-stationarity, the authors use the Henriksson and Merton (1981) model, which is expressed as:

$$R_{pt} - R_{ft} = \alpha_T + \beta_1 X_t + \beta_2 Y_t + \varepsilon_{pt} \tag{1}$$

where: $X_t = R_{mt} - R_{ft}$ and $Y_t = \max[0, -(R_{mt} - R_{ft})]$; R_{mt} is the return on the market portfolio.; $\beta_2 Y_t$ measures the market timing ability of a manager; and Y_t captures the down market premium.

Results show that international funds exhibit good security selection ability and high overall performance. Over the five-year period from 1989-93 the funds have a positive monthly excess return of 0.09% with six out of the ten European funds reporting positive average selectivity coefficients. In contrast, most European fund managers do not display good market timing ability. Managers of Pacific funds have the most impressive performance. Nine out of the eleven managers have positive selectivity ability, with three being statistically significant.

In summary, international fund managers are weak market timers. Also, consistent with evidence from domestic funds, there is a negative correlation between a manager's selection and market timing abilities.

Ahmed, P., P. Gangopadhyay and S. Nanda, 2003, "Investing in Emerging Market Mutual Funds," *Journal of Business and Economic Perspectives*, 29, 5-15.

This article addresses the performance of open-end stock and bond emerging market mutual funds conditional on the monetary policy regime in the U.S. Over the early nineties cash inflows into emerging market funds averaged 15% growth annually, which is largely attributable to institutional investment. By 1999 U.S. based open-end mutual funds had nearly $35 billion invested in emerging markets.

The authors examine the performance of 191 emerging market stock and bond funds over the period 1980-2000 conditional on U.S. monetary policy. Results show that emerging market stock funds underperform their corresponding country indices, as evidenced by their lower returns, higher risk, and lower Sharpe ratios. Among the categories of funds, Latin American funds have the highest Sharpe and Treynor ratios, while Diversified Emerging Market funds (investing in Pacific and Latin American countries) have the next highest Sharpe and Treynor ratios and the highest Jensen alpha. Emerging market bond funds perform in line with their benchmarks.

Results further indicate that emerging market stock funds have higher returns and Sharpe ratios in restrictive monetary policy periods than during expansionary periods. Emerging market stock funds have higher Sharpe ratios than the corresponding indexes during restrictive periods, but have lower Sharpe ratios than their indexes during expansive periods. Similarly, the Jensen alphas of all but the Latin American funds are positive during periods of restrictive U.S. monetary policy. Diversified Emerging Market and Asia Pacific funds exhibit the largest differences in mean returns between the restrictive and expansive policy regimes. The authors report that emerging market bond funds perform better in restrictive monetary policy periods, and have higher Sharpe ratios than their benchmarks during these periods.

6.4 Bond Funds

Blake, C., E. Elton and M. Gruber, 1993, "The Performance of Bond Mutual Funds," *The Journal of Business*, 66, 371-403.

This paper is the first major study on the performance of bond funds. It uses a sample of 46 non-municipal bond funds (excluding money market funds) identified as "bond" or "specialized" in the 1979 edition of *Weisenberger's Investment Companies*. Fund performance is measured using single-index, three-index, and six-index models. Various benchmark indexes selected to evaluate performance include: Lehman Brothers government/corporate bond index, Lehman Brothers mortgage-backed securities, Blume/Keim high-yield index, Lehman Brothers intermediate bond, and Lehman Brothers long-term government bond.

Results show that the average annual alphas across the different models varies from -0.28% to -0.83%. Out of the 46 funds, between 27 and 33 funds report negative alphas. The paper also examines the predictability of alphas from various models using the fund's past alpha to a naïve forecasting model that assumes a fund's future alpha to equal its past. All tests indicate that no model is useful in predicting the future.

Philpot, J., D. Hearth, J. Rimbey, and C.T. Schulman, 1998, "Active Management, Fund Size, and Bond Mutual Fund Returns," *The Financial Review*, 33, 115-126.

This study investigates management effectiveness in bond mutual funds by examining the relation between fund returns and individual fund attributes that represent management activity. The study estimates the relationship between 27 bond funds' performance and six independent variables using a multiple regression model:

$$RETURN_{it} = \beta_0 + \beta_1(RETURN_{-1,it}) + \beta_2(EXPENSE_{,it}) +$$
$$\beta_3(TURNOVER_{it}) + \beta_4(ASSETS_{it}) + \quad (1)$$
$$\beta_5(LOAD_{it}) + \beta_6(DISTFEE_{it}) + \sum_{1}^{8} \omega_t D_t + \varepsilon_{it}$$

where: $RETURN_{it}$ = Sharpe ratio for fund i in time t, RETURN-1 = lagged Sharpe ratio, EXPENSE = total expense ratio, TURNOVER = five year average portfolio turnover, ASSETS = natural log of funds total assets, LOAD = a dummy variable for load, DISTFEE = a dummy variable for 12b-1 fees, ω_t = time period t's dummy variable coefficient, and D_t = a dummy variable denoting the time period.

Results show that fund performance is unrelated to past performance. There appear to be economies of scale with the ASSETS coefficient being significant and positive. Performance is negatively related to both expense ratio and portfolio turnover. Finally, bond funds with no loads outperform those with loads, and funds with 12b-1 fees perform better than those without. Their findings support the conventional wisdom that bond funds are fairly homogeneous and that individual fund managers do not have much opportunity to distinguish themselves.

Detzler, M., 1999, "The Performance of Global Bond Mutual Funds," *Journal of Banking and Finance*, 23, 1195-1217.

This paper is among the first to study the risk and return characteristics of global bond funds. The author examines the risk - return characteristics of 19 global funds for the period 1988-95 by testing if the funds outperform various bond benchmarks. He also investigates whether these funds provide diversification benefits for

U.S. investors, and the relationship between expenses and performance.

Two single-index and three multi-index benchmarks are employed. The single-index benchmarks are the Salomon Brothers World Government Bond Index and the Salomon Brothers Broad Index, which includes U.S. Government and corporate issues. The multi-index models use benchmarks incorporating excess returns in local currencies on five government bond indices: Canada, Germany, Japan, UK, and the US, as well as the following currencies: Canadian dollar, German mark, Japanese yen, and British pound.

The average excess returns on the 19 funds range from 0.08% to 0.39%, averaging 0.23% per month. Standard deviations range from 1.45% to 2.99%. Results show that the average Jensen measures for the funds range from -0.08 to -0.01. On average the funds do not outperform any of the five benchmarks, suggesting that active management strategies do not benefit investors. The regression of the funds' Jensen measures on expense ratios show a significant negative relationship. For four out of the five benchmark models, every one dollar in expense reduces performance by more than one dollar.

6.5 Socially Responsible Funds

Hamilton, S., H. Jo, and M. Statman, 1993, "Doing Well While Doing Good? The Investment Performance of Socially Responsible Mutual Funds," *Financial Analysts Journal*, 49, 62-66.

This is one of the first studies to evaluate the performance of socially responsible funds. The authors test three alternative hypotheses: (1) the expected returns of socially responsible portfolios are equal to those of conventional portfolios; (2) the expected returns of socially responsible portfolios are lower than those of conventional portfolios; and (3) the expected returns of stocks of socially responsible portfolios are higher than the expected returns of conventional portfolios.

Using a combined sample of 32 equity mutual funds (1981-1990), the authors report mean excess returns for conventional funds of -1.68% annually, compared to a -0.76% return for the corresponding group of 17 socially responsible funds. The mean excess return of another conventional group of funds is -0.5% per year, which is higher than but not statistically different from the return of -3.33% for a corresponding group of 15 socially responsible mutual funds.

The study concludes that the market does not price social responsibility characteristics and that investors can expect to lose nothing by investing in socially responsible mutual funds.

Goldreyer, E., P. Ahmed, and D. Diltz, 1999, "The Performance of Socially Responsible Mutual Funds: Incorporating Sociopolitical Information in Portfolio Selection," *Managerial Finance*, 25, 25-40.

The authors examine 49 mutual funds (equity, bond, and balanced) that screen their investments for corporate performance with regard to social goals or policies, and compare the performance of these firms to a sample of conventional funds. This study also partitions the sample into funds that use "inclusion" screens versus those that do not employ such screening.

They explain how incorporating sociopolitical information in portfolio decisions may affect returns. For example, the conventional wisdom in the investment arena is best described by the phrase, "Don't mix money and morality." In contrast, social activists have argued that firms with good social records will be more valuable, as socially responsible firms are likely to have less litigation and worker turnover, thus reducing operating costs.

However, academics argue that this added constraint is not likely to affect investors' overall return. This group asserts that with: (1)

the large number of publicly traded firms available, (2) the low transactions costs associated with equities trading, and (3) the rapid flow of information through equities markets, the added sociopolitical constraint is not usually binding. Thus, the effect of augmenting portfolio decisions with sociopolitical information is an empirical issue.

The authors report that socially responsible funds neither consistently outperform nor underperform conventional mutual funds. However, they do find that socially responsible funds employing inclusion screens outperform the sample that does not employ such screening. They conclude that social screening does not affect the investment performance of mutual funds in any systematic or predictable way.

Statman, M., 2000, "Socially Responsible Mutual Funds," *Financial Analyst Journal*, 56, 30-39.

In this work the author analyzes the performance of the Domini Social Index (DSI), an index of socially responsible companies and socially responsible mutual funds, using both raw returns and risk-adjusted returns for the period 1990-98. Statman employs a matched sample (on size) of 62 conventional funds and 31 socially responsible mutual funds with the S&P 500 and DSI as benchmarks. Although the socially responsible funds' expense ratio of 1.5% closely matches the 1.56% ratio for the conventional funds, the mean performance of the socially responsible funds is marginally better than that of the control funds. The author notes that the DSI performs marginally better than the S&P 500 Index in raw returns, but slightly worse in risk-adjusted terms. He concludes that investors who care about social responsibility can build on Sharpe's extended CAPM by including value-expressive components as determinants of investment demand and expected returns.

PAPERS REVIEWED IN CHRONOLOGICAL ORDER

Cumby, R. and J. Glen, 1990, "Evaluating the Performance of International Mutual Funds," *The Journal of Finance*, 45, 497-521.

Blake, C., E. Elton and M. Gruber, 1993, "The Performance of Bond Mutual Funds," *The Journal of Business*, 66, 371-403.

Hamilton, S., H. Jo, and M. Statman, 1993, "Doing Well While Doing Good? The Investment Performance of Socially Responsible Mutual Funds," *Financial Analysts Journal*, 49, 62-66.

Gallo, J. and P. Swanson, 1996 "Comparative Measures of Performance for U.S.-Based International Equity Mutual Funds," *Journal of Banking and Finance*, 20, 1635-1650.

Kao, G., L. Cheng, and K. Chan, 1998, "International Mutual Fund Selectivity and Market Timing During Up and Down Market Conditions," *The Financial Review*, 33, 127-144

Philpot, J., D. Hearth, J. Rimbey, and C.T. Schulman, 1998, "Active Management, Fund Size, and Bond Mutual Fund Returns," *The Financial Review*, 33, 115-126.

Detzler, M., 1999, "The Performance of Global Bond Mutual Funds," *Journal of Banking and Finance*, 23, 1195-1217.

Ackermann, C., R. McEnally, and D. Ravenscraft, 1999, "The Performance of Hedge Funds: Risk, Retrun and Incentives," *The Journal of Finance*, 54, 833-874.

Liang, B., 1999, "On the Performance of Hedge Funds," *Financial Analysts Journal,* 55, 72-85.

Brown, S., W. Goetzmann, and R. Ibbotson, 1999, "Offshore Hedge Funds: Survival and Performance, 1989-95," *The Journal of Business*, 72, 91-117.

Goldreyer, E., P. Ahmed, and D. Diltz, 1999, "The Performance of Socially Responsible Mutual Funds: Incorporating Sociopolitical Information in Portfolio Selection," *Managerial Finance*, 25, 25-40.

Statman, M., 2000, "Socially Responsible Mutual Funds," *Financial Analyst Journal*, 56, 30-39.

Liang, B., 2001, "Hedge Fund Performance: 1990-1999," *Financial Analysts Journal,* 57, 11-19.

Ahmed, P., P. Gangopadhyay and S. Nanda, 2003, "Investing in Emerging Market Mutual Funds," *Journal of Business and Economic Perspectives*,29,5-15.

7. OTHER ISSUES

7.1 Introduction

This chapter is eclectic in the subject matter of the articles summarized. Generally, the issues addressed are unique, and they differ from those broad topics addressed in the earlier chapters. The topics range from fund risk in bull versus bear markets, to the number of mutual funds that constitute a diversified fund portfolio, to mutual fund risk-taking as a response to incentives.

Fabozzi, F. and J. Francis, 1979, "Mutual Fund Systematic Risk for Bull and Bear Markets: An Empirical Examination," *The Journal of Finance*, 34, 1243-1250.

The authors explain that if beta nonstationarity exists, then the use of an estimated beta for the entire period can give different conclusions about manager skill under varying market conditions. To test whether a fund's alpha intercept or beta risk measure differs statistically in bull or bear markets, the authors estimate equations under both market conditions. Three definitions of bull and bear markets are used with monthly returns for 85 mutual funds to determine whether betas differ in up or down markets. The authors report that the number of funds exhibiting a significant shift in beta over time is not statistically different from the number of random portfolios exhibiting a parameter shift. When alpha is considered, the percentage found to be significant is not different than would be expected under normal sampling theory. The authors conclude that their work extends the findings of Treynor and Mazury (1966) by presenting additional evidence that fund managers do not shift their fund's beta to take advantage of market movements.

Veit, E. and J. Cheney, 1982, "Are Mutual Funds Market Timers?" *The Journal of Portfolio Management*, Winter, 35-42.

This paper investigates the effectiveness of mutual fund managers' market timing decisions. The authors define a successful timing strategy as: (1) correctly forecasting "bull" and "bear" markets, and (2) making appropriate changes in the fund's risk exposure in anticipation of forecasted market movements. To test the null hypothesis that funds' alphas and betas are the same in both up and down markets, the authors employ annual returns of 74 funds (income, growth, and balanced) for the period 1944-1978. They analyze two types of portfolio revision decisions: (1) when the fund allocates resources to each identified category: cash, fixed income, and common stocks, and (2) when the fund alters the allocation of resources within each category. For classifying "bull" versus "bear" market periods, the authors use four different schemes of market return classifications. They report that average betas and alphas do not change significantly in up or down markets for the various schemes overall. A large majority of funds demonstrate unsuccessful timing. They conclude that their market timing model yields evidence of an efficient capital market.

Dermine, J., D. Neven, and J. Thisse, 1991, "Towards an Equilibrium Model of the Mutual Funds Industry," *Journal of Banking and Finance*, 15, 485-499.

In this paper the authors model the mutual fund industry wherein each fund is allowed to select the characteristics of its portfolio and examine whether overall investment opportunities are improved. They assume a single period, mean-variance world, with perfect information and model competition between funds as a non-cooperative Nash-equilibrium in a simultaneous game. In

Section II of the paper the demand for fund shares is derived in an industry comprising two underlying traded securities, one risk-free and one risky, which may be purchased directly by investors. Funds select portfolios consisting of these two securities, and it is this selection with which the model is primarily concerned. In Section III the market equilibrium and its properties are analyzed. Competition is modeled as a non-cooperative game in which all funds simultaneously choose their portfolios to profit-maximize. The outcome of this process is a non-competitive Nash-equilibrium where fund strategies are the percentage of the risky security in their portfolios (at least four funds must exist). The main message of their model is that the possibility to combine various mutual funds or underlying securities increases competition in the mutual fund industry. In the conclusion the authors explain that they have shown that a non-cooperative equilibrium exists where the industry is split into two groups: money market funds and funds holding the market portfolio.

Elton, E., M. Gruber, S. Das, and M. Hlavka, 1993, "Efficiency with Costly Information: A Reinterpretation of Evidence from Managed Portfolios," *The Review of Financial Studies*, 6, 1-22.

In this article the authors discuss the differences between the findings of Ippolito (1989) and those of earlier researchers. Ippolito reports non-negative alphas to the actions of informed managers and finds that frictions such as fees, turnover, and expenses are not associated with inferior returns. These findings contrast with Jensen (1968) and other earlier researchers who report negative alphas.

Elton, et al., view mutual funds as combinations of three portfolios: one containing S&P stocks, one containing non-S&P stocks, and one containing bonds. They reexamine returns over previously tested periods, taking into account the performance of non-S&P assets. They report that holding non-S&P stocks would cause negative alphas for funds over the earlier period studied by Jensen and others, and positive alphas over the period studied by Ippolito. Bonds are not found to have much portfolio impact.

When considering the issues of market efficiency, turnover, and expenses, the authors again adjust for non-S&P assets. They examine the relationship between performance and three cost variables: expense ratios, turnover, and load costs. They find that fund managers underperform passive portfolios and that funds with higher fees/turnover underperform those with lower fees/turnover. They conclude that adjusting for non-S&P equities results in Ippolito's findings being similar to those in earlier studies.

Shukla, R. and S. Singh, 1994, "Are CFA Charterholders Better Equity Fund Managers?" *Financial Analysts Journal*, 50, 68-74.

The authors discuss that the Chartered Financial Analyst (CFA) designation is a premier professional qualification that requires serious study of ethical and professional standards, securities law and regulation, financial accounting, economics, fixed-income and equity-securities, and portfolio management. The paper asks a simple question, "Does a portfolio manager's advanced professional education, such as a CFA designation, result in superior fund performance?"

Using a sample of equity mutual funds for the period July 1988 to December 1992, the authors find that funds managed by at least one CFA-designated manager perform better than funds managed by individuals without the charter. The funds managed by CFA-designated managers are more diversified and often more risky. However, the performance difference between managers is not always statistically significant.

Del Guercio, D., 1996, "The Distorting Effect of the Prudent-man Laws on Institutional Equity Investments," *Journal of Financial Economics,* 40, 31-62.

The author briefly reviews the legal background of the prudent-man rule and examines the impact of such constraints on institutional investment manager behavior. Del Guercio examines portfolio holdings of 941 managers who hold over 4,000 equities valued at $1.1 trillion to determine if sector tilting exists across manager types. The findings show that on average bank managers invest 31% of their equity portfolio in the highest quality stocks (ranked $A+$ by S&P) compared to mutual funds that invest only 15% of portfolio holdings in these stocks. Relative to market value-weightings, banks invest an extra $21 billion and funds $5 billion less than would be expected. The author concludes that prudent-man laws distort the incentives of institutional managers to act in the best interest of their clients.

Khorana A., 1996, "Top Management Turnover: An Empirical Investigation of Mutual Fund Managers," *Journal of Financial Economics,* 40, 403-427.

Khorana hypothesizes an inverse relation between the probability of managerial change and the fund's past performance as measured by: (1) asset growth rate, and (2) objective and risk-adjusted returns. For a logit analysis he uses a sample of 339 funds that experienced managerial replacement and a control sample of 4,830 funds matched by investment objective over the period 1979-1992. He reports significantly different portfolio returns as well as different mean asset growth rates of 89% and 51% for the control and replacements samples, respectively. A significantly larger increase in expenses and turnover rates is also seen for the replacements sample relative to the control. The author concludes that his findings are consistent with a well-functioning internal and external market mechanism for fund managers.

Falkenstein, E., 1996, "Preferences for Stock Characteristics as Revealed by Mutual Fund Portfolio Holdings," *The Journal of Finance,* 51, 111-135.

This paper primarily investigates the revealed preferences of mutual funds for various stock characteristics. Using *Morningstar* data on portfolio holdings of 2,261 funds (1992-1993), the author examines the cross-section of the fund sector's percentage ownership of given securities traded on the NYSE and the AMEX. The paper also addresses tests of herd behavior via the implications of the various stocks held. The empirical results of the paper are: (1) funds display a preference for highly-volatile stocks; (2) funds tend to avoid low-price stocks (less than \$5 per share); (3) funds show an aversion to small-company stocks (except for the small-cap sector); (4) funds avoid stocks characterized by few newspaper articles; and (5) funds avoid stocks that have only recently been exchange listed.

The breakdown of mutual funds by sector, age, and size, suggests that fund preferences, except for firm size, are generally consistent across all fund sectors (growth, growth-income, small-company, equity-income, balanced, and aggressive-growth). Results also identify that several of these variables imply that herding into these stocks occurs at various times. The author posits that as stocks acquire specific characteristics, mutual funds are more likely to hold them; thus the evidence for herding. The author concludes that share price level, volatility, liquidity, news articles, age, and size, are all significant in explaining aggregate fund holdings of individual securities.

Chevalier, J. and G. Ellison, 1997, "Risk Taking by Mutual Funds as a Response to Incentives," *Journal of Political Economy*, 105, 1167-1200.

In this paper the authors explore the risk-taking behavior of mutual funds in light of the agency relationship between funds and customers. To do so, they first examine the relationship between fund performance and investment inflows, and then they examine how portfolios are altered toward the end of the year. The purpose of this process is to gain insight in risk changes, thereby allowing an assessment of whether funds are reactive to identified incentives. Their analysis of the flow-performance relationship allows them to derive estimates of how the market compensates funds for altering the riskiness of their portfolios toward year-end as a function of the funds' first nine-month performance, age, and other attributes.

A data set of 398 funds (3,036 fund years) for the period 1983-1993 is divided into "old" (ages six-plus years) and "new" (ages two to five years) for comparison purposes. They find that large returns bring significantly higher inflows as a fund begins to come to the attention of relatively uninformed investors and that larger funds appear to grow more slowly than other funds. Chevalier and Ellison also discuss how the flow-performance relationship may induce funds to alter their portfolio riskiness toward year-end. They find that flows into older funds are less sensitive to recent performance than those into younger funds, but that across all funds the relationship holds. The authors conclude that funds alter their portfolios in the final quarter of the year in a manner consistent with the September incentive to take risk calculated from the flow-performance relationship.

O'Neal, E., 1997, "How Many Mutual Funds Constitute a Diversified Mutual Fund Portfolio?" *Financial Analysts Journal,* March, 37-46.

In reviewing various diversification issues, the author focuses on Radcliff's (1994) terminal wealth standard deviation (TWSD), which is the standard deviation of resulting terminal-wealth levels. The author employs 168 growth and growth-and-income funds (1976-1994) to perform simulations for examining the impact of holding various numbers of funds on the expected variability of an investor's terminal wealth. The three choice variables are: fund objective, holding period (5, 10, 15, or 19 years), and number of funds. A strategy of investing in a single fund is used as a baseline. In simulations one dollar is invested at the beginning of the holding period and is equally divided among randomly chosen funds. At the end of each quarter rebalancing occurs until the end of the period. O'Neal also considers three measures of downside risk: shortfall probability, mean shortfall, and semivariance. On the basis of the simulations, the author concludes that the traditional measure of volatility (time-series standard deviation) is not greatly influenced by holding multiple funds, but that the TWSD is significantly reduced by a declining degree as additional funds are held. Also, two of the three downside risk measures considered are substantially reduced by including multiple funds in a portfolio.

Goetzmann, W. and N. Peles, 1997, "Cognitive Dissonance and Mutual Fund Investors," *The Journal of Financial Research,* 20, 145-158.

The authors briefly discuss the mystery of why some investors stay with mutual funds that consistently perform poorly. They explain that investors may adjust their beliefs to support past decisions and that this tendency to justify past actions exemplifies the psychological phenomenon of cognitive dissonance. Closely related to this phenomenon is that of the "endowment" effect often attributed to the perception that people believe something they own is superior to something they do not own. To address these issues they present evidence from questionnaire responses of mutual fund investors about their recall of past fund performance. (The analysis allows a differentiation between an endowment effect and beliefs conditional upon past choices.) Samples of investors are from two groups: (1) members of a state chapter of the American Association of Individual Investors, and (2) a group of professional architects who have a profit-sharing plan and who also invest in mutual funds. The questionnaire used has several questions, including one which asks for an estimate of the prior year's fund return and its relative performance. Subjects are also asked how many years of poor performance would be necessary before they would switch funds.

Their findings suggest that the cognitive processes used by investors for inaction are based on biased past performance beliefs. Also, investors have a higher opinion of their personal choice, as might be expected. Survivorship bias is controlled by the inclusion of defunct funds. Investors appear to respond to the performance of the lowest quartile funds no differently than to those in the second and third quartiles. Thus, although the market rewards the top performers, it does little to discipline poor performers. In summary, the authors conclude that even well-informed investors tend to bias their perceptions about past performance. Although some investors hold biased beliefs, the authors report that the number of investors in poor funds is small. The authors contend that if new investors focus on past performance rankings, mutual fund companies might benefit by increasing the number and variability of funds under management.

Collins, S. and P. Mack, 1997, "The Optimal Amount of Assets under Management in the Mutual Fund Industry," *Financial Analysts Journal,* 53, 70-71.

Collins and Mack briefly discuss how mutual funds have recently become major competitors for household savings, with nearly $3 trillion in assets under management. They reference Sirri and Tufano (1998), who report that mutual fund complexes may be able to achieve scale economies and efficiencies in areas such as shareholder services, research, transactions, and other operations. They employ data on expenses and net assets for 533 fund complexes with assets totaling $2 trillion as of 1994. The data comprise three distinct product groups: bond funds, equity funds, and money funds. Firms with assets exceeding $10 billion account for almost 75% of total assets. The authors report that complexes achieve scale efficiencies in the following asset ranges: bond fund complexes with assets of $4 - $6 billion, equity fund complexes with assets of $600 - $800 million, and money fund complexes of $10 - $12 billion. They conclude that a full-service fund complex managing $20 - $40 billion may attain full economies of scale.

Tufano, P. and M. Sevick, 1997, "Board Structure and Fee-setting in the U.S. Mutual Fund Industry," *Journal of Financial Economics,* 46, 321-355.

The authors discuss the fiduciary duties of boards and how characteristics such as board size and independent member participation can affect a board's decision-making and effectiveness. Two particularly interesting features of mutual fund boards are: (1) the clearly defined board responsibilities of selecting managers and setting fees for the fund management company, and (2) the fact that members usually serve on multiple fund boards. They note that a majority of independent directors must approve all advisory and distribution contracts.

To study governance practices the authors construct a data base of the funds offered by the 50 fund sponsors with the most assets under management as of 1992. The sample accounts for 69% of all U.S. open-end fund assets. They describe the structure of fund boards along several dimensions: (1) board size, (2) percentage of board occupied by independent directors, (3) number of the particular sponsor boards on which individuals sit, and (4) compensation received for service. They analyze the cross-sectional relationship between fees charged by funds and board structure after holding constant fund size, sponsor size, distribution method, and performance history, among other factors.

The authors report evidence of economies of scale at the fund level, but only limited evidence of such economies at the sponsor level. There is a positive relationship between fund age and fees, suggesting that more experienced funds charge higher fees. Fees vary significantly among funds with different objectives, as well as those with different distribution channels and different clienteles. Shareholder fees are lower when fund boards are smaller, have a larger fraction of independent directors, and are composed of directors who sit on more boards of the fund sponsors' other funds. There is some evidence that boards with higher director fees approve higher shareholder fees. The authors offer a caveat in that this work is about the relative effectiveness of different types of mutual fund boards; whereas we must also be concerned with the absolute effectiveness of boards in protecting shareholder interests.

Brown, K.C., W.V. Harlow, and L.T. Starks, 1998, "Of Tournaments and Temptations: An Analysis of Managerial Incentives in the Mutual Fund Industry," *Journal of Finance*, 51, 85-110.

The authors explain that even without incentive fee contracts, the competitive nature of the mutual fund industry alone can adversely effect the portfolio decisions made by a fund manager. The paper presents the managerial decision process as akin to a "tournament" in which all funds having comparable investment objectives compete with one another. Similar to any sporting event, the amount of remuneration that a fund receives depends on the performance of the fund relative to other funds in the universe. In such a tournament type framework, managers attempting to maximize their expected compensation may revise the composition of their portfolios to "make up" for losses incurred in the past.

This paper tests the hypothesis that managers of investment portfolios manipulate their fund risk contingent upon the overall performance of funds. Funds that are mid-year "losers" tend to increase their fund volatility more than the mid-year "winners." The authors test the hypothesis that:

$$(\sigma_{2L} / \sigma_{1L}) > (\sigma_{2W} / \sigma_{1W}) \tag{1}$$

where the subscripts L and W represent the interim loser and winner strategies, and the subscripts 1 and 2 denote the first and second subperiods. This equation implies that the risk adjustment ratio for the interim losers will be greater than those for interim winners.

Using monthly returns from more than 330 growth oriented mutual funds over the 1980-1991 period, the paper shows that losers (winners) do indeed shift their investments so as to increase risk by a greater (lesser) degree. This effect is more pronounced in the later half of the sample as investor awareness escalates. These risk changes are also shown to be due to explicit managerial actions and not generated entirely as a result of change in asset levels. The results show that the fund industry, by focusing so much attention to annual performance, may be effectively changing managerial objectives from long-term to short-term perspectives.

Arteaga, K., C. Ciccotello, and T. Grant, 1998, "New Equity Funds: Marketing and Performance," *Financial Analysts Journal,* 54, 43-49.

The authors explain two strategies that fund sponsors use to introduce new equity funds and to promote these funds after introduction: (1) "incubation," which allows a fund to compile a private favorable track record and then to be marketed to the public, and (2) "selective attention," which directs favorable allocations of "special situations" into new funds that are available to the public. To perform their investigation they utilize a data base containing 741 aggressive-growth funds and 619 growth and income funds taken from the *Alexander Steele Mutual Fund Data Base.* The authors ask two questions: (1) Does the investment objective of the new fund affect the sponsor's marketing strategy? and (2) Do the new fund marketing strategies offer public investors superior return opportunities? They test two hypotheses:

> H1: First full-year new-fund performance is not different from established fund performance.

> H2: The probability that funds have superior performance in their second years of operation

if they have superior first-year performance is
not different from 50%.

Results indicate that aggressive-growth new funds outperform
established funds in their first year, but that the superior performance
does not continue. However, fewer than half of the growth and
income new funds exceed median established fund returns. Findings
indicate that incubation and selective attention strategies are not
commonly used with growth and income funds. When considering
second-year performance, they find that the first-year aggressive
growth fund winners are likely to become average second-year
performers. For investors seeking superior returns they must invest
as soon as possible during the first year with selective attention
funds. However, these funds' early success tends to be followed by
relatively poor returns. In the case of incubator funds, all are found
to be winners during their first year of operation when they are very
small. After the first year of operation, they experience rapid growth
and do not attain returns significantly different from those of
established funds. Neither group offers superior returns other than
temporally.

Alexander, G., J. Jones, and P. Nigro, 1998, "Mutual Fund
Shareholders: Characteristics, Investor Knowledge, and Sources of
Information," *Financial Services Review,* 7, 301-316.

The authors examine responses from a survey (contracted by the
SEC and OCC) of 2,000 randomly selected mutual fund investors
who bought shares from six various distributors. The survey
collected two kinds of data: (1) data on demographics, financial, and
fund ownership attributes of fund shareholders, and (2) data on
mutual investors' familiarity with costs, investment risk, and sources
of information. They report the following:

- Broker and direct fund customers are more likely to be college educated than other channel users, such as bank customers.
- The fund prospectus is the most widely used source of information (57.7% of respondents), followed by employer-provided material (44.5%), newspaper/magazines (42%), friends (37.6%), and work presentations (33.5%).
- Most fund investors know that it is possible to lose money in stock, bond, and money market funds.
- Fewer than one in five respondents estimates fund expenses closely.
- Only a slight positive relationship is expected between current and future performance.
- Financial literacy is higher for prospectus users compared to investors using other sources of information.

The authors conclude that the goal of better educated investors would be best served by a joint effort among plan sponsors, brokers, fund companies, and regulatory agencies.

Barclay, M., N. Pearson, and M. Weisbach, 1998, "Open-end Mutual Funds and Capital Gains Taxes," *Journal of Financial Economics,* 49, 3-43.

This paper examines, from both theoretical and empirical perspectives, the question of how funds choose a capital gains realization policy, which determines gains overhangs. The authors first discuss some irregularities about capital gains realizations by funds from 1976-1992. After explaining how funds are taxed under Subchapter M of the tax code, the authors state that funds should realize capital gains to the extent that they are offset by capital losses. However, most funds do not follow such a policy, as evidenced by stock and long-term bond funds that realize an average of 38.6% and 25.5%, respectively. They explain that existing shareholders and potential new shareholders have different capital gains preferences: (1) existing investors would prefer to defer gains, thereby creating a large, unrealized gains overhang, and (2) new investors would prefer funds without large overhangs of gains for obvious tax reasons. The authors note that a portfolio's capital gains are particularly costly to investors when a fund contracts because of net redemptions.

The authors consider a model wherein the manager of a mutual fund attempts to attract finite-lived investors via an optimal capital gains realization policy, and employ a sample of 2,434 funds for analysis. Results reveal that, not surprisingly, stock funds have higher capital gains yields than do bond funds, and that capital gains yields are higher for: funds with higher returns, older funds, growing funds, and funds with high turnover rates. They also find properties of overhangs that are consistent with their model of funds attempting to maintain a "target" overhang. After discussing the relation between overhang and expected growth rates, growth rate volatility, and return volatility, they report that overhang is positively related to estimated growth rate and return volatility, and negatively related to growth rate volatility and income yield. They also find that funds marketed to institutional (tax-exempt) investors have larger overhangs than do other funds.

Livingston, M. and E. O'Neal, 1998, "The Cost of Mutual Fund Distribution Fees," *The Journal of Financial Research*, 21, 205-218.

The authors explain that distribution fees, in contrast to management fees and turnover costs, are unique because several arrangements have evolved in the industry for paying these fees. The paying of these fees comprises three categories: (1) front-end load (when shares are purchased), (2) back-end load (when shares are redeemed), and (3) annual fees (12b-1 fees). They note that 64% of domestic equity funds charge distribution fees, of which

23% have front-end and annual fees, 22% have back-end and annual fees, 11% have only annual fees, and 7% have only front-end fees. The authors develop a discount formula which expresses the present value of fees as a percentage of original investment, thereby allowing ease of comparison of fees between investment choices. Livingston and O'Neal show that structurally similar arrangements can produce a wide range of costs to investors. Whether or not an investor knows the expected holding period, this analysis has value as an input into the investment decision. The authors conclude that investors should purchase the class of shares having the lowest present value of distribution costs.

Chevalier, J, and G. Ellison, 1999, "Are Some Mutual Fund Managers Better Than Others? Cross Sectional Patterns in Behavior and Performance," *Journal of Finance*, 54, 875-899.

This paper examines the relationship between mutual fund performance and the characteristics of the fund mangers. In particular the paper studies the relationship between performance and the manager's age, average SAT scores at the manager's undergraduate institution, and whether the manager has an MBA.

The authors use a sample of 492 managers who had sole responsibility for a growth or growth and income fund for at least part of the period 1988-94. The study looks cross-sectionally at how performance is related to observable characteristics of fund managers. A simple regression of market excess returns on managerial characteristics shows that managers with MBAs outperform managers without MBAs by 63 basis points per year, and younger managers on average outperform older ones. The most robust performance difference is attributed to the average composite SAT scores of the managers' undergraduate institutions.

The coefficients of SAT scores and age are significant at the 1% level and the MBA coefficient at the 11% level. For example, managers who attend the fourth highest SAT score school outperform managers from the mean SAT school by one percentage point per year. A manager who is one year older than another is expected to achieve a return that is 8.6 basis points lower. Controlling for either risk or expense is not sufficient to explain the superior performance of managers from higher SAT schools.

Keim D., 1999, "An Analysis of Mutual Fund Design: The Case of Investing in Small-cap Stocks," *Journal of Financial Economics,* 51, 173-194.

Keim examines the "9-10 Fund," a passive mutual fund launched in 1982 based on the CRSP small-cap 9-10 Index. The fund, although passive, pursues a strategy by employing portfolio-weighted trading strategies and cost-minimizing investment rules. The fund's traders participate in the upstairs market, hence applying liquidity and thus enjoying negative trade costs. A number of securities in the 9-10 Index are systematically excluded from the portfolio, including: (1) ADRs and foreign stocks, (2) REITs and closed-end funds, (3) limited partnerships and bankrupt firms, and (4) non-National Market System stocks and stocks with less than four market makers.

The author decomposes the return difference between the 9-10 Fund and the 9-10 Index as: (1) return difference due to investment rules, and (2) return difference due to trading strategies. The paper reports that the total return difference comprises: 15, 5, and 4 basis points due to investment rules, trading strategies, and CRSP 9-10 Index construction, respectively. He concludes that over the 1982-1995 period the fund delivered the price behavior of small-cap stocks (correlation of 0.98) while providing an annual premium of 2.2% over the index.

Eichberger, J., S. Grant, and S. King, 1999, "On Relative Performance Contracts and Fund Manager's Incentives," *European Economic Review*, 43, 135-161.

The authors explain that fund managers often seem to adopt similar investment strategies and offer that one explanation may be found in relative performance reward schemes. Recent research contends that comparative performance evaluation can only improve agent-manager performance and that in a worst case scenario a principal can revert to the non-contingent contract. However, a criticism of these results is that the models do not capture: (1) the complexity of the manager's task, or (2) the importance of uncoordinated decisions by more than one principal. In a managed fund investors face a two-stage incentive problem: (1) requiring managers to investigate relevant investment options, and (2) requiring managers to choose a suitably risky portfolio. The authors explain that investors must allow for the fact that other owners may be pursuing similar strategies.

Their model assumes two independent funds in the analysis of how the naïve use of relative performance evaluation may lead to unintended managerial behavior: (1) too little or too much risk-taking, and (2) herding. If owners realize that there occur simultaneous lettings of relative performance contracts, then they will not utilize such contracts. The authors conclude that their analysis of the impossibility of symmetric relative performance contracts is the major contribution of this work.

Carpenter, J. and A. Lynch, 1999, "Survivorship Bias and Attrition Effects in Measures of Performance Persistence," *Journal of Financial Economics*, 54, 337-374.

In this work the authors simulate standard tests of mutual fund performance persistence under varying assumptions about return-generating processes, survival criteria, and availability of data. The authors explain that among various studies of survivorship bias and performance persistence, Carhart (1997) finds the strongest performance persistence in a complete sample of funds, and the weakest in the survivor-biased sample.

For their simulations the authors generate samples of fund alphas with three different return-generating processes: One process has no true persistence, while the alternative processes introduce persistence with either independent alphas, reflecting differences in ability, or with zero-mean alphas that represent a "hot-hands" phenomenon. The number of funds is 213, similar to that of Carhart. They also generate samples with no attrition and samples with missing returns. The authors test for persistence by measuring the performance of decile portfolios ranked on past returns, contingency tables, and cross-sectional regressions of alphas on prior alphas. The comparison of their findings with those of Carhart's returns, which are generated with real fund data, suggests that U. S. mutual fund performance is persistent, but that the generating process is not captured by their persistence specifications. They conclude that their results support prior findings that mutual fund performance is truly persistent.

Fant, L. and E. O'Neal, 2000, "Temporal Changes in the Determinants of Mutual Fund Flows," *Journal of Financial Research,* 23, 353-371.

The authors discuss how the mutual fund marketplace has undergone substantial development and changes in recent years, with high growth rates for both equity and bond fund accounts, net assets, and numbers of individual funds. They note how recent studies have reported that investors reward funds with high performance but do not punish funds with poor performance.

Some prior studies have investigated the flow of money into funds as a function of fund attributes.

In this paper the authors explore whether changes in the nature of the mutual fund marketplace have altered the way aggregate investors select mutual funds. These changes include an increase in the number of funds available, an increase in the no-load clientele, and an increase in regular investment plans. To compute fund flows (all new money invested plus reinvested distributions) they employ data for the period 1977-1993. In examining the changing relationship between fund flows and prior performance, they divide the sample into four sub-periods. They find that fund flows generally increase across time and across quintiles. Using a piecewise regression, they find that the asymmetric fund flow-performance reported by earlier studies still holds. The reward to high-performing funds is seen to increase over the sample period, while poor performers do not experience divestment activity. They conclude that, in spite of the availability of fund information, the increase in fund advertisement, and the increased availability of performance evaluation services, investors' sensitivity to fund performance is essentially unchanged.

Ahmed, P., 2001, "Forecasting Correlation Among Equity Mutual Funds," *Journal of Banking and Finance*, 26, 1187-1208.

This study distills estimates of future mutual fund return correlations using past returns by comparing eight models which are grouped into three major categories: historical, mean, and index models. Funds in each model period are stratified by their style class in the manner of Gallo and Lockwood (1997). The author explains that a model may predict correlations between funds of a certain style (intra-style) but fail to do so for funds in different style categories (inter-style). This study compares the forecasting ability of each model in intra- and inter-style sub-samples and compares these results with those of a holdout sample to determine the efficacy of each model.

To estimate future correlations the author computes pairwise correlations over a historical period. The historical model computes correlations from the historical time-series returns of each fund. The mean model computes mean pairwise correlations from the historical correlation matrix and treats this mean as a forecast of the future pairwise correlation between all pairs of funds. With the third class of models, the index models, it is assumed that securities move together because of their response to a set of common factors.

Results indicate that the multi-index and the three-factor models using the three Fama-French factors are the best performing models and are the most consistent in their relative ranks when comparing different forecasting periods and different forecasting lengths. The author concludes that the success of these models is consistent across sub-samples of funds in the same or different style categories.

Elton, E., M. Gruber and C. Blake, 2001, "A First Look at the Accuracy of CRSP Mutual Fund Database and a Comparison of the CRSP and Morningstar Mutual Fund Databases," *Journal of Finance*, 56, 2415-2430.

Most studies of mutual funds are empirical in nature and frequently employ databases provided by the Center for Research in Security Prices (CRSP) and *Morningstar*. This paper examines the potential errors in the databases by comparing the return data in the CRSP database to the Morningstar data.

The *Morningstar* database has a well known survivorship bias because it contains only data for funds that are in operation. This bias in the *Morningstar* database causes performance measures to be inflated by between 40 basis points and 1%. Such a survivorship bias can appear to make fund performance predictable when none is present.

The CRSP database in contrast, while free from survivorship bias, has another bias that the authors label as "omission bias." The omission bias in the CRSP database arises because the return data on CRSP files is monthly for some funds, annual for others, and for some funds no returns are recorded. The monthly CRSP data understates the proportion of mergers and liquidations and thus overstates performance. One way to avoid the omission bias is to restrict the sample of funds studied to only those funds that have over \$15 million in total net assets at the beginning of any observation period.

Davis, J.L., 2001, "Mutual Fund Performance and Manager Style," *Financial Analysts Journal*, 57, 19-27.

This study examines the relationship between equity fund performance and manager style. Two issues are examined: First, does any particular investment style deliver abnormal performance, and second, is there any evidence of performance persistence?

The study uses a sample consisting of 4,686 funds covering 26,564 fund-years from 1962-1998. Fund styles are identified using the Fama-French three- factor model:

$$R_{i,t} - R_{f,t} = \alpha_i + \beta_i(R_{m,t} - R_{f,t}) + \chi_i SMB_t + \gamma_i HML_t + \varepsilon_{i,t} \quad (1)$$

where: SMB stands for returns of small minus big size stocks, and HML stands for returns of high minus low book-value stocks.

Funds are placed into a style portfolio at the beginning of each year from 1965 to 1998 with returns from the previous 36 months used to estimate pre-formation slopes. Based on these slopes, funds are allocated to similar style portfolios. Results show that growth funds perform better than value funds independent of their market capitalization.

PAPERS REVIEWED IN CHRONOLOGICAL ORDER

Fabozzi, F. and J. Francis, 1979, "Mutual Fund Systematic Risk for Bull and Bear Markets: An Empirical Examination," *The Journal of Finance*, 34, 1243-1250.

Veit, E. and J. Cheney, 1982, "Are Mutual Funds Market Timers?" *The Journal of Portfolio Management*, Winter, 35-42.

Dermine, J., D. Neven, and J. Thisse, 1991, "Towards an Equilibrium Model of the Mutual Funds Industry," *Journal of Banking and Finance*, 15, 485-499.

Elton, E., M. Gruber, S. Das, and M. Hlavka, 1993, "Efficiency with Costly Information: A Reinterpretation of Evidence from Managed Portfolios," *The Review of Financial Studies*, 6, 1-22.

Shukla, R. and S. Singh, 1994, "Are CFA Charterholders Better Equity Fund Managers?" *Financial Analysts Journal*, 50, 68-74.

Del Guercio, D., 1996, "The Distorting Effect of the Prudent-man Laws on Institutional Equity Investments," *Journal of Financial Economics,* 40, 31-62.

Khorana A., 1996, "Top Management Turnover: An Empirical Investigation of Mutual Fund Managers," *Journal of Financial Economics,* 40, 403-427.

Falkenstein, E., 1996, "Preferences for Stock Characteristics as Revealed by Mutual Fund Portfolio Holdings," *The Journal of Finance,* 51, 111-135.

Chevalier, J. and G. Ellison, 1997, "Risk Taking by Mutual Funds as a Response to Incentives," *Journal of Political Economy,* 105, 1167-1200.

O'Neal, E., 1997, "How Many Mutual Funds Constitute a Diversified Mutual Fund Portfolio?" *Financial Analysts Journal,* March, 37-46.

Goetzmann, W. and N. Peles, 1997, "Cognitive Dissonance and Mutual Fund Investors," *The Journal of Financial Research,* 20, 145-158.

Collins, S. and P. Mack, 1997, "The Optimal Amount of Assets under Management in the Mutual Fund Industry," *Financial Analysts Journal,* 53, 70-71.

Tufano, P. and M. Sevick, 1997, "Board Structure and Fee-setting in the U.S. Mutual Fund Industry," *Journal of Financial Economics,* 46, 321- 355.

Brown, K.C., W.V. Harlow, and L.T. Starks, 1998, "Of Tournaments and Temptations: An Analysis of Managerial Incentives in the Mutual Fund Industry," *Journal of Finance*, 51, 85-110.

Arteaga, K., C. Ciccotello, and T. Grant, 1998, "New Equity Funds: Marketing and Performance," *Financial Analysts Journal,* 54, 43-49.

Alexander, G., J. Jones, and P. Nigro, 1998, "Mutual Fund Shareholders: Characteristics, Investor Knowledge, and Sources of Information," *Financial Services Review,* 7, 301-316.

Barclay, M., N. Pearson, and M. Weisbach, 1998, "Open-end Mutual Funds and Capital Gains Taxes," *Journal of Financial Economics,* 49, 3-43.

Livingston, M. and E. O'Neal, 1998, "The Cost of Mutual Fund Distribution Fees," *The Journal of Financial Research*, 21, 205-218.

Chevalier, J, and G. Ellison, 1999, "Are Some Mutual Fund Managers Better Than Others? Cross Sectional Patterns in Behavior and Performance," *Journal of Finance*, 54, 875-899.

Keim D., 1999, "An Analysis of Mutual Fund Design: The Case of Investing in Small-cap Stocks," *Journal of Financial Economics,* 51, 173-194.

Eichberger, J., S. Grant, and S. King, 1999, "On Relative Performance Contracts and Fund Manager's Incentives," *European Economic Review,* 43, 135-161.

Carpenter, J. and A. Lynch, 1999, "Survivorship Bias and Attrition Effects in Measures of Performance Persistence," *Journal of Financial Economics*, 54, 337-374.

Fant, L. and E. O'Neal, 2000, "Temporal Changes in the Determinants of Mutual Fund Flows," *Journal of Financial Research,* 23, 353-371.

Ahmed, P., 2001, "Forecasting Correlation Among Equity Mutual Funds," *Journal of Banking and Finance*, 26, 1187-1208.

Elton, E.J., M.J. Gruber and C.R. Blake, 2001, "A First Look at the Accuracy of CRSP Mutual Fund Database and a Comparison of the CRSP and Morningstar Mutual Fund Databases," *Journal of Finance*, 56, 2415-2430.

Davis, J.L., 2001, "Mutual Fund Performance and Manager Style," *Financial Analysts Journal*, 57, 19-27.

.

ENDNOTES

[1] See Krooss and Blyn (1971), p. 201.

[2] Much of this chapter is adapted from Anderson and Born (1992).

[3] See Roll (1978).

[4] Readers may wish to refer to the pioneering work on modern portfolio theory by Markowitz (1952).

[5] See Treynor (1965). The Treynor ratio is shown to be ratio of the risk premium to the systematic risk of the portfolio.

[6] The quadratic regression framework of Treynor and Mazuy (1966) posits that market timers should make more money when the market rises or falls dramatically.

[7] See Report of the Committee on Interstate and Foreign Commerce (House Report #2247 [August, 1962]).

BIBLIOGRAPHY

A Study of Mutual Funds, House Report #2247 [August, 1962], Report of the Committee on Interstate and Foreign Commerce.

Ackermann, C., R. McEnally, and D. Ravenscraft, 1999, "The Performance of Hedge Funds: Risk, Return and Incentives," *The Journal of Finance*, 54, 833-874.

Ahmed, P., 2001, "Forecasting Correlation Among Equity Mutual Funds," *Journal of Banking and Finance*, 26, 1187-1208.

Ahmed, P., P. Gangopadhyay and S. Nanda, 2003, "Investing in Emerging Market Mutual Funds," *Journal of Business and Economic Perspectives*, 29, 5-15.

Alexander, G., J. Jones, and P. Nigro, 1998, "Mutual Fund Shareholders: Characteristics, Investor Knowledge, and Sources of Information," *Financial Services Review,* 7, 301-316.

Anderson, S. and J. Born, Closed-End Investment Companies: Issues and Answers. Hingham, MA: Kluwer Academic Publishers, 1991.

Anderson, S., B. Coleman, D. Gropper, and H. Sunquist, 1996, "A Comparison of the Performance of Open- and Closed-end Investment Companies," *Journal of Economics and Finance*, 20, 3-11.

Arteaga, K., C. Ciccotello, and T. Grant, 1998, "New Equity Funds: Marketing and Performance," *Financial Analysts Journal,* 54, 43-49.

Barclay, M., N. Pearson, and M. Weisbach, 1998, "Open-end Mutual Funds and Capital Gains Taxes," *Journal of Financial Economics,* 49, 3-43.

Becker C., W. Ferson, D. Myers, and M. Schill, 1999, "Conditional Market Timing with Benchmark Investors," *Journal of Financial Economics,* 52, 119-148.

Bhattacharya, S. and P. Pfleider, <u>A Note on Performance Evaluation, Technical Report, 714.</u> Stanford University, Stanford California. 1983.

Blake, C., E. Elton and M. Gruber, 1993, "The Performance of Bond Mutual Funds," *The Journal of Business,* 66, 371-403.

Bogle, J., 1998, "The Implications of Style Analysis for Mutual Fund Performance Evaluation," *The Journal of Portfolio Management,* Summer, 34-42.

Brown, F. and D. Vickers, 1963, "Mutual Fund Portfolio Activity, Performance, and Market Impact," *The Journal of Finance,* 18, 377-391.

Brown, K., W. Harlow and L. Starks, 1998, "Of Tournaments and Temptations: An Analysis of Managerial Incentives in the Mutual Fund Industry," *The Journal of Finance,* 51, 85-110.

Brown, S. and W. Goetzmann, 1995, "Performance Persistence," *The Journal of Finance,* 50, 679-698.

Brown, S. and W. Goetzmann, 1997, "Mutual Fund Styles," *Journal of Financial Economics,* 43, 373-399.

Brown, S., W. Goetzmann, and R. Ibbotson, 1999, "Offshore Hedge Funds: Survival and Performance, 1989-95," *The Journal of Business*, 72, 91-117.

Carhart, M., 1997, "On Persistence in Mutual Fund Performance," *The Journal of Finance*, 52, 57-82.

Carlson, R., 1970 "Aggregate Performance of Mutual Funds, 1948-1967," *Journal of Financial and Quantitative Analysis,* 1-32.

Carpenter, J. and A. Lynch, 1999, "Survivorship Bias and Attrition Effects in Measures of Performance Persistence," *Journal of Financial Economics*, 54, 337-374.

Chance, D. and S. Ferris, 1991, "Mutual Fund Distribution Fees: An Empirical Analysis of the Impact of Deregulation," *Journal of Financial Services Research*, 5, 25-42.

Chang, E. and W. Lewellen, 1984, "Market Timing and Mutual Fund Investment Performance," *The Journal of Business*, 57, 57-72.

Chevalier, J. and G. Ellison, 1997, "Risk Taking by Mutual Funds as a Response to Incentives," *Journal of Political Economy,* 105, 1167-1200.

Chevalier, J, and G. Ellison, 1999, "Are Some Mutual Fund Managers Better Than Others? Cross Sectional Patterns in Behavior and Performance," *Journal of Finance*, 54, 875-899.

Chordia, T., 1996, "The Structure of Mutual Fund Charges," *Journal of Financial Economics*, 41, 3-39.

Close, J., 1952, "Investment Companies: Closed-End versus Open-End," *Harvard Business Review*, 29, 79-88.

Collins, S. and P. Mack, 1997, "The Optimal Amount of Assets under Management in the Mutual Fund Industry," *Financial Analysts Journal*, 53, 70-71.

Cumby, R. and J. Glen, 1990, "Evaluating the Performance of International Mutual Funds," *The Journal of Finance*, 45, 497-521.

Davis, J.L., 2001, "Mutual Fund Performance and Manager Style," *Financial Analysts Journal*, 57, 19-27.

Del Guercio, D., 1996, "The Distorting Effect of the Prudent-man Laws on Institutional Equity Investments," *Journal of Financial Economics*, 40, 31-62.

Dellva, W. and G. Olson, 1998, "The Relationship Between Mutual Fund Fees and Expenses and Their Effects on Performance," *Financial Review*, 33, 85-103.

Dermine, J., D. Neven, and J. Thisse, 1991, "Towards an Equilibrium Model of the Mutual Funds Industry," *Journal of Banking and Finance*, 15, 485-499.

Detzler, M., 1999, "The Performance of Global Bond Mutual Funds," *Journal of Banking and Finance*, 23, 1195-1217.

DiBartolomeo, D. and E. Witkowski, 1997, "Mutual Fund Misclassification: Evidence Based on Style Analysis," *Financial Analysts Journal*, (September/October), 32-43.

Droms, W. and D. Walker, 2001, "Persistence of Mutual Fund Operating Characteristics: Returns, Turnover Rates, and Expense Ratios," *Applied Financial Economics*, 11, 457-466.

Edelen, R., 1999, "Investor Flows and the Assessed Performance of Open-end Mutual Funds," *Journal of Financial Economics,* 53, 439-466.

Edwards, F. and X. Zhang, 1998, "Mutual Funds and Stock and Bond Market Stability," *The Journal of Financial Services Research,* 13, 257-282.

Eichberger, J., S. Grant, and S. King, 1999, "On Relative Performance Contracts and Fund Manager's Incentives," *European Economic Review,* 43, 135-161.

Elton, E., M. Gruber, S. Das, and M. Hlavka, 1993, "Efficiency with Costly Information: A Reinterpretation of Evidence from Managed Portfolios," *The Review of Financial Studies*, 6, 1-22.

Elton, E., M. Gruber and C. Blake, 2001, "A First Look at the Accuracy of CRSP Mutual Fund Database and a Comparison of the CRSP and Morningstar Mutual Fund Databases," The Journal of Finance, 56, 2415-2430.

Fabozzi, F. and J. Francis, 1979, "Mutual Fund Systematic Risk for Bull and Bear Markets: An Empirical Examination," *The Journal of Finance*, 34, 1243-1250.

Falkenstein, E., 1996, "Preferences for Stock Characteristics as Revealed by Mutual Fund Portfolio Holdings," *The Journal of Finance*, 51, 111-135.

Fant, L., 1999, "Investment Behavior of Mutual Fund Shareholders: The Evidence from Aggregate Fund Flows," *The Journal of Financial Markets,* 2, 391-402.

Fant, L. and E. O'Neal, 1999, "Do You Need More Than One Manager for a Given Equity Style? Evidence from Mutual Funds," *The Journal of Portfolio Management,* Summer, 68-75.

Fant, L. and E. O'Neal, 2000, "Temporal Changes in the Determinants of Mutual Fund Flows," *Journal of Financial Research,* 23, 353-371.

Ferris, S. and D. Chance, 1987, "The Effect of 12b-1 Plans on Mutual Fund Expense Ratios: A Note," *The Journal of Finance,* 42, 1077-1082.

Ferson, W. and V. Warther, 1996, "Evaluating Fund Performance in a Dynamic Market," *Financial Analysts Journal,* 52, 20-28.

Ferson, W. and R. Schadt, 1996, "Measuring Fund Strategy and Performance in Changing Economic Conditions," *The Journal of Finance,* 51, 425-461.

Gallo, J. and L. Lockwood, 1997, "Benefits of Proper Style Classification of Equity Portfolio Managers," *The Journal of Portfolio Management,* 23, 47-55.

Gallo, J. and L. Lockwood, 1999, "Fund Management Changes and Equity Style Shifts," *The Journal of Portfolio Management,* 55, 44-52.

Gallo, J. and P. Swanson, 1996 "Comparative Measures of Performance for U.S.-Based International Equity Mutual Funds," *Journal of Banking and Finance*, 20, 1635-1650.

Goetzmann, W. and N. Peles, 1997, "Cognitive Dissonance and Mutual Fund Investing," *Journal of Financial Research,* 20, 145-158.

Goetzmann, W. and R. Ibbotson, 1994, "Do Winners Repeat? Patterns in Mutual Fund Return Behavior," *The Journal of Portfolio Management,* Winter, 9-18.

Goldreyer, E., P. Ahmed, and D. Diltz, 1999, "The Performance of Socially Responsible Mutual Funds: Incorporating Sociopolitical Information in Portfolio Selection," *Managerial Finance*, 25, 25-40.

Grant, D., 1977, "Portfolio Performance and the 'Cost' of Timing Decisions," *The Journal of Finance*, 32, 837-846.

Grinblatt, M. and S. Titman, 1989, "Mutual Fund Performance: An Analysis of Quarterly Portfolio Holdings," *The Journal of Business,* 62, 393-416.

Grinblatt, M. and S. Titman, 1993, "Performance Measurement without Benchmarks: An Examination of Mutual Fund Returns," *The Journal of Business,* 66, 47-68.

Grinblatt, M., S. Titman and R. Wermers, 1995, "Momentum Investment Strategies, Portfolio Performance, and Herding: A Study of Mutual Fund Behavior," *American Economic Review,* 85, 1088-1105.

Gruber, M., 1996, "Another Puzzle: The Growth in Actively Managed Mutual Funds," *The Journal of Finance*, 51, 783-810.

Hamilton, S., H. Jo, and M. Statman, 1993, "Doing Well While Doing Good? The Investment Performance of Socially Responsible Mutual Funds," *Financial Analysts Journal*, 49, 62-66.

Harless, D. and S. Peterson, 1998, "Investor Behavior and the Persistence of Poorly-performing Mutual Funds," *Journal of Economic Behavior and Organization,* 37, 257-276.

Hendricks, D., J. Patel, and R. Zeckhauser, 1993, "Hot Hands in Mutual Funds: Short-run Persistence of Relative Performance, 1974-1988," *The Journal of Finance,* 43, 93-130.

Hendricks, D., J. Patel, and R. Zeckhauser, 1997, "The J-shape of Performance Persistence Given Survivorship Bias," *Review of Economics and Statistics*, 79, 161-166.

Herman, E., 1963, "Mutual Fund Management Fee Rates," *The Journal of Finance*, 18, 360-376.

Huddart, S., 1999, "Reputation and Performance Fee Effects on Portfolio Choice by Investment Advisers," *Journal of Financial Markets,* 2, 227-271.

Indro, D., C. Jiang, M. Hu, and W. Lee, 1999, "Mutual fund Performance: Does Size Matter?" *Financial Analysts Journal*, 55, 74-87.

Ippolito, R., 1992, "Consumer Reaction to measures of Poor Quality: Evidence from the Mutual Fund Industry," *Journal of Law and Economics,* 35, 45-70.

Jagannathan, R. and R. Korajczyk, 1986, "Assessing the Market Timing Performance of Managed Portfolios," *The Journal of Business*, 59, 217-235.

Jain, P. and J. Wu, 2000, "Truth in Mutual Fund Advertising: Evidence on Future Performance and Fund Flows," *The Journal of Finance*, 55, 937-958.

Jensen, M., 1968, "The Performance of Mutual Funds in the Period 1945-1964," *The Journal of Finance,* 23, 389-416.

Kahn, R. and A. Rudd, 1995, "Does Historical Performance Predict Future Performance?" *Financial Analysts Journal*, 51, 43-52.

Kao, G., L. Cheng, and K. Chan, 1998, "International Mutual Fund Selectivity and Market Timing During Up and Down Market Conditions," *The Financial Review*, 33, 127-144.

Keim, D., 1999, "An Analysis of Mutual Fund Design: The Case of Investing in Small-cap Stocks," *Journal of Financial Economics,* 51, 173-194.

Khorana A., 1996, "Top Management Turnover: An Empirical Investigation of Mutual Fund Managers," *Journal of Financial Economics,* 40, 403-427.

Kihn, J., 1996, "To Load or Not to Load? A Study of Marketing and Distribution Charges of Mutual Funds," *Financial Analysts Journal*, (May/June), 28-36.

Krooss H. and M. Blyn, A History of Financial Intermediaries. New York: Random House, 1971

Kon, S., 1983, "The Market-Timing Performance of Mutual Fund Managers," *The Journal of Business*, 56, 323-347.

Kon, S. and F. Jen, 1979, "The Investment Performance of Mutual Funds: An Empirical Investigation of Timing, Selectivity and Market Efficiency," *The Journal of Business*, 52, 263-289.

Lehmann, B. and D. Modest, 1987, "Mutual Fund Performance Evaluation: A Comparison of Benchmarks and Benchmark Comparisons," *The Journal of Finance*, 42, 233-265.

Lettau M., 1997, "Explaining the Facts with Adaptive Agents: The Case of Mutual Fund Flows," *Journal of Economic Dynamics and Control*, 21, 1117-1147.

Liang, B., 1999, "On the Performance of Hedge Funds," *Financial Analysts Journal*, 55, 72-85.

Liang, B., 2001, "Hedge Fund Performance: 1990-1999," *Financial Analysts Journal*, 57, 11-19.

Livingston, M. and E. O'Neal, 1998, "The Cost of Mutual Fund Distribution Fees," *The Journal of Financial Research*, 21, 205-218.

Lunde, A., A. Timmermann, and D. Blake, 1999, "The Hazards of Mutual Fund Underperformance: A Cox Regression Analysis," *Journal of Empirical Finance*, 6, 121-152.

Malhotra, D. and R. McLeod, 1997, "An Empirical Analysis of Mutual Fund Expenses," *The Journal of Financial Research,* 20, 175-190.

Markowitz, H., 1952, "Portfolio Selection," *The Journal of Finance*, 12, 71-91.

Malkiel, B., 1995, "Returns from Investing in Equity Mutual Funds: 1971-1991," *The Journal of Finance,* 50, 549-572.

McDonald, J., 1974, "Objectives and Performance of Mutual Funds, 1960-1969," *Journal of Financial and Quantitative Analysis,* 311-333.

McLeod, R. and D. Malhotra, 1994, "A Re-examination of the Effect of 12b-1 Plans on Mutual Fund Expense Ratios," *The Journal of Financial Research*, 17, 231-240.

Miller, T. and N. Gressis, 1980, "Nonstationarity and Evaluation of Mutual Fund Performance," *Journal of Financial and Quantitative Analysis*, 15, 639-654.

Najand, M. and L. Prather, 1999, "The Risk Level Discriminatory Power of Mutual Fund Investment Objectives: Additional Evidence," *Journal of Financial Markets,* 2, 307-328.

O'Neal, E., 1997, "How Many Mutual Funds Constitute a Diversified Mutual Fund Portfolio?" *Financial Analysts Journal*, March, 37-46.

O'Neal, E., 1999, "Mutual Fund Share Classes and Broker Incentives," *Financial Analysts Journal,* 55, 76-87.

Philpot, J., D. Hearth, J. Rimbey, and C.T. Schulman, 1998, "Active Management, Fund Size, and Bond Mutual Fund Returns," *The Financial Review*, 33, 115-126.

Roll, R., 1978, "Ambiguity When Performance is Measured by the Security Market Line," *The Journal of Finance* 33, 1059-69.

Ross, S., 1976, "The Arbitrage Theory of Capital Asset Pricing," *Journal of Economic Theory*, 13, 341-360.

Santini, D. and J. Aber, 1998, "Determinants of Net New Money Flows to the Equity Mutual Fund Industry," *Journal of Economics and Business,* 50, 419-429.

Sharpe, W., 1992, "Asset Allocation: Management Style and Performance Management," *Journal of Portfolio Management*, 18, 7-19.

Sharpe, W., 1966, "Mutual Fund Performance," *The Journal of Business,* 39, 119-138.

Shukla, R. and S. Singh, 1994, "Are CFA Charterholders Better Equity Fund Managers?" *Financial Analysts Journal*, 50, 68-74.

Sirri, E., and P. Tufano, 1998, "Costly Search and Mutual Fund Flows," *The Journal of Finance,* 53, 1589-1622.

Smith, K., 1978, "Is Fund Growth Related to Fund Performance?" *The Journal of Portfolio Management,* 5, 49-54.

Starks, L., 1987, "Performance Incentive Fees: An Agency Theoretic Approach," *Journal of Financial and Quantitative Analysis*, 22, 17-32.

Statman, M., 2000, "Socially Responsible Mutual Funds," *Financial Analyst Journal*, 56, 30-39.

Treynor, J, 1965, "How to Rate Management of Investment Funds," *Harvard Business Review*, 63-75.

Treynor, J. and K. Mazury, 1966, "Can Mutual Funds Outguess the Market?" *Harvard Business Review*, July, 131-136.

Trzcinka, C., 1995, "Equity Style Classifications: Comment," *The Journal of Portfolio Management, Spring*, 44-46.

Tufano, P. and M. Sevick, 1997, "Board Structure and Fee-setting in the U.S. Mutual Fund Industry," *Journal of Financial Economics,* 46, 321- 355.

Veit, E. and J. Cheney, 1982, "Are Mutual Funds Market Timers?" *The Journal of Portfolio Management*, Winter, 35-42.

Volkman, D., 1999, "Market Volatility and Perverse Timing Performance of Mutual Fund Managers," *The Journal of Financial Research*, 22, 449-470.

Wermers, R., 2000, "Mutual Fund Performance: An Empirical Decomposition into Stock-Picking Talent, Style, Transactions Costs, and Expenses," *Journal of Finance*, 55, 1655-1695.

Warther, V., 1997, "Aggregate Mutual Fund Flows and Security Returns," *Journal of Financial Economics,* 39, 209-235.

Zheng, L., 1999, "Is Money Smart? A Study of Mutual Fund Investors' Fund Selection Ability," *The Journal of Finance*, 54, 632-665.

INDEX